THE

POCKET
IDIOT'S
GUIDE™ TO

French
Phrases

Second Edition

by Gail Stein

A L P H A

A member of Penguin Group (USA) Inc.

ALPHA BOOKS

Published by the Penguin Group

Penguin Group (USA) Inc., 375 Hudson Street, New York, New York 10014, U.S.A.

Penguin Group (Canada), 10 Alcorn Avenue, Toronto, Ontario, Canada M4V 3B2 (a division of Pearson Penguin Canada Inc.)

Penguin Books Ltd, 80 Strand, London WC2R 0RL, England

Penguin Ireland, 25 St Stephen's Green, Dublin 2, Ireland (a division of Penguin Books Ltd)

Penguin Group (Australia), 250 Camberwell Road, Camberwell, Victoria 3124, Australia (a division of Pearson Australia Group Pty Ltd)

Penguin Books India Pvt Ltd, 11 Community Centre, Panchsheel Park, New Delhi—110 017, India

Penguin Group (NZ), cnr Airborne and Rosedale Roads, Albany, Auckland 1310, New Zealand (a division of Pearson New Zealand Ltd)

Penguin Books (South Africa) (Pty) Ltd, 24 Sturdee Avenue, Rosebank, Johannesburg 2196, South Africa

Penguin Books Ltd, Registered Offices: 80 Strand, London WC2R 0RL, England

International Standard Book Number: 1-59257-182-4
Library of Congress Catalog Card Number: 2003113812

08   07   8

Interpretation of the printing code: The rightmost number of the first series of numbers is the year of the book's printing; the rightmost number of the second series of numbers is the number of the book's printing. For example, a printing code of 04-1 shows that the first printing occurred in 2004.

Printed in the United States of America

Note: This publication contains the opinions and ideas of its author. It is intended to provide helpful and informative material on the subject matter covered. It is sold with the understanding that the author and publisher are not engaged in rendering professional services in the book. If the reader requires personal assistance or advice, a competent professional should be consulted.

The author and publisher specifically disclaim any responsibility for any liability, loss, or risk, personal or otherwise, which is incurred as a consequence, directly or indirectly, of the use and application of any of the contents of this book.

Most Alpha books are available at special quantity discounts for bulk purchases for sales promotions, premiums, fund-raising, or educational use. Special books, or book excerpts, can also be created to fit specific needs.

For details, write: Special Markets, Alpha Books, 375 Hudson Street, New York, NY 10014.

This book is dedicated to my patient, proofreader husband, Douglas; my skilled computer consultant son, Eric; my most ardent fan and son, Michael; to my parents, Sara and Jack Bernstein, whose love and support have helped me to become the woman I am today; and to my sister, Susan Opperman, who got all the art genes, my brother-in-law, Jay, who makes sure I stay warm, and Zachary, my precocious nephew.

Contents

Introduction

In today's fast-growing, ever-expanding, multi-cultural world the acquisition of at least one foreign language is a must for both business and pleasurable pursuits. If you're traveling, working, or just a student at heart, you may want or need an intensive crash course or a simple brush-up in French. The time to do it is *now!*

Learning French will allow you to enter a world of endless opportunities, intriguing experiences, and exciting challenges. Learning French will provide you with the key that opens the door to a different lifestyle, a distinctive culture, and a unique, romantic outlook on life. Learning French will give you a valuable tool that will serve you well when you least expect it. Open up your mind and immerse yourself in this wonderful experience. Study French with patience and love and the rewards you reap will be boundless.

What's Inside

So you're curious about French and that's why you've picked up this book! Learning this popular Romance language is a very practical thing to do because it's used internationally: It's spoken on all seven continents throughout the world. Wherever your travels may take you, you'll find that a knowledge of French will prove invaluable and will greatly enrich your experiences.

Now if you're like most of us, you want to achieve quick and easy results with a minimum amount of work. Well, then this is the book for you. You'll painlessly and effortlessly learn all about pronunciation and grammar without having to sacrifice speed and accuracy. Students, travelers, and business people alike will find all the basics, in addition to common daily vocabulary and expressions that are useful in every conceivable situation. A wide range of topics is presented: food, clothing, health, leisure activities, business terms, and much more.

This book is not a just phrase book, a travel guide, or a foreign language text. What makes *The Pocket Idiot's Guide to French Phrases, Second Edition,* unique is that it compactly combines all three of these elements: It gives those who want an extremely good working command of French an extremely useful tool. In no time flat, you'll understand and be understood in French with ease and enjoyment. There'll be no embarrassment and no frustration. Yes, learning French can be fun!

Extras to Help You Along

Besides the idiomatic expressions, helpful phrases, lists of vocabulary words, and down-to-earth grammar, this book has useful information provided in sidebars throughout the text.

Full Speed Ahead

This box tells you how to work with French grammar easily, or reminds you of rules you might have forgotten from previous chapters.

Attention!

This box tells you how to avoid making a mistake.

An Extra Workout

This box gives you a chance to practice what you've learned. These tips will help you begin to put your French skills to use.

Acknowledgments

Thank you! Thank you! Thank you to some very special people who have made a difference in my life and have greatly enriched it.

A special: "I love you!" accompanied by hugs and kisses to:

Ray Elias for getting my program up and running, for ensuring that the local bookstores keep Stein in stock, and for being an even greater guy 38 years later; Werner Elias for making a very important delivery, for which I will be eternally grateful; Roger H. Herz for being a dear friend and a cooperative consultant; Marty Hyman for giving me the best legal advice imaginable; Marty Leder for making me laugh and keeping my spirits up; Chris Levy for being the best advisor and confidante in the world, for always knowing the right thing to do, and for teaching me lessons I needed to learn; and Michael Koch for giving me his help, support, and input.

I would also like to acknowledge the contributions, input, support, and interest of the following people:

Natercia Alves, Marie-Claire Antoine, Monika Bergenthal, Vivian Bergenthal, Richard Calcasola of Maximus Hair Salon, Nancy Chu, Trudy Edelman, Richard Edelman, Barbara Gilson, Robert Grandt, François Haas of the Office of the French Treasury, Nancy Lasker of L'Oréal, Max Rechtman, Marie-Madeleine Saphire, Barbara Shevrin, and Billy Fields and the Alpha production team.

Trademarks

marks have been appropriately capitalized. Alpha Books and Penguin Group (USA) Inc. cannot attest to the accuracy of this information. Use of a term in this book should not be regarded as affecting the validity of any trademark or service mark.

The Quickest and Easiest Pronunciation Guide

Now, before you jump into the chapters and accompanying exercises, familiarize yourself with the pronunciation guide in this section. It's really quite simple to sound irresistibly French especially if you were lucky enough to have been born with a "good ear." If you can carry a tune or play a musical instrument you should have no trouble at all imitating the lilt, intonation, and stress of the language. Just follow these fast and easy steps:

- Lose your inhibitions immediately and put on your best French accent. Don't be afraid to ham it up!

- Allow yourself to slip and slide the sounds together while speaking the language.

- Use your nose wisely for the correct pronunciation of French nasal sounds.

- Remember that some French accents change the sound of the letter on which they appear.

- Understand that practice and devotion will help improve your accent. Be patient!

Stress

In French, each syllable of a word has just about equal stress, so when speaking, try to pronounce each syllable of a word with equal emphasis. When you remember, place a slightly stronger emphasis on the last syllable of a group of words. Speak smoothly, speak musically, and speak evenly. My best advice: For maximum results, stay on an even keel.

A Liaison or an Elision?

Liaison (linking) and *elision* (sliding) are two linguistic elements of the French language that give it its fluidity and melodious beauty.

Liaison refers to the linking of the final consonant of one word with the beginning vowel of the next word.

> Vousarrivez   *voo zah-ree-vay*

Attention!

The one thing that you really want to avoid is overstress. Do not overemphasize letters, words, or syllables. This will target you as a novice and will ruin the sounds of the language.

Elision occurs when there are two pronounced vowel sounds: one at the end of a word, and the other at the beginning of the next word. The first vowel is dropped and replaced by an apostrophe. Simply slide the words together:

| Je + arrive | J'arrive | *zah-reev* |
| le + hôtel | l'hôtel | *lo-tehl* |

Accent Marks

Think of accent marks as pronunciation guideposts that will help you speak like an old pro. There are five different accent marks in French that may be used to change the sounds of letters (*é* versus *è*, *a* versus *â*, and so on), to differentiate between the meanings of two words whose spellings are otherwise the same (*a* meaning *has* versus *à* meaning *to* or *at*; *ou* meaning *or* versus *où* meaning *where*, and so on), or to replace an *s* that was part of the word many centuries ago in old French.

- An *accent aigu* (´) is seen only on an *e* (é).

  é produces the sound (*ay*), as in *day*.

- An *accent grave* (`) is used with *a* (à), *e* (è), and *u* (ù).

  On an *e*, an accent grave produces the sound of (*eh*) as the *e* in the English word *met*. It doesn't change the sound of the *a* (à) or *u* (ù).

- An accent *circonflexe* (^) may be used on all vowels: *â, ê, î, ô, û*. The vowel sounds are longer for *â* and *ô*, are slightly longer for *ê*, and are imperceptible on *î* and *û*.

- A *cédille* (ˌ) is used only on a *c* (ç). When the ç comes before *a*, *o*, or *u*, it means that you pronounce the letter as a soft *c* (the sound of *s*).

- A *tréma* (¨) occurs on a second vowel in a series. This accent indicates that the two vowels are pronounced separately, each having its own distinct sound: Haïti (*ay-ee-tee*), Noël (*noh-ehl*).

French vowels are a bit complicated because each one has a number of different sounds, and there are specific rules and accent marks that help you determine how the vowel should be pronounced.

The *é* may replace an *s* that used to exist in the word in old French. Adding a mental *s* immediately after *é* may enable you to easily determine the meaning of a word. See if the meaning jumps out at you: *éponge* (as in *sponge*), *étranger* (as in *stranger*)

This circumflex also often replaces an *s* from old French. Simply stick a mental *s* in the word to see if the meaning jumps out at you: *arrêter* (as in *arrest*), *fête* (as in *feast*, *festival*).

French Letter	Symbol	Pronunciation Guide
a, à, â	ah	Say *a* as in sp*a*. Open wide and say ahhh …
é, final *er*, and *ez;* es in some one-syllable words; a few ai; et combinations; é are always pronounced *ay*.	ay	Say *ay* as in d*ay*.

French Letter	Symbol	Pronunciation Guide
e in one-syllable words or in the middle of a word followed by a single consonant	uh	Say *e* as in th*e*.
è, ê, and e (plus two consonants or a final pronounced consonant) et, ei, ai	eh	Say *e* as in m*e*t.
i, î, y, ui	ee	Say *i* as in magaz*i*ne.
i + ll il when preceded by a vowel	y	Say *y* as in *y*our. For the ill, ail, or eil combinations, remember to keep the l silent.
i + ll in these words only	eel	Say the word *eel*.

Every rule has an exception; or in this case, because there aren't too many, the words might be worth memorizing—especially because they're used frequently.

ville (*veel*)   million (*mee-lyohN*)

village (*vee-lahzh*)   tranquille (*trahN-keel*)

mille (*meel*)

French Letter	Symbol	Pronunciation Guide
o (before se), o (last pronounced sound of, word) ô, au, eau	o	Say *o* as in n*o*. Keep your lips rounded.
o when followed by a pronounced consonant other than s	oh	Say *o* as in l*o*ve.
ou, où, oû	oo	Say *oo* as in t*oo*th.
oy, oi	wah	Say *w* as in *w*atch.

You may be tempted to pronounce *oi* like *oy*, as the sound heard at the beginning of the word *oyster*. Avoid the pitfall. Practice the correct *wa* sound until you get it down pat.

French Letter	Symbol	Pronunciation Guide
u, û	ew	No equivalent

There really is no English sound equivalent to the French *u* sound. Try the following: Say the sound *oo* as in *Sue* while trying to say *ee* as in *see*. As you try to make the sound, concentrate on puckering your lips as if you just ate a very sour pickle. That's about as close as you can get.

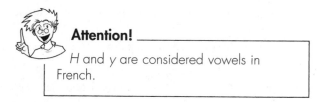

Attention!

H and *y* are considered vowels in French.

The Nose Knows

Nasal sounds will occur when a vowel is followed by a single *n* or *m* in the same syllable. In the pronunciation guide, you will see a vowel sound followed by *N*. This indicates that you must make a nasal sound.

French Nasal	Symbol	Pronunciation Guide
an (am), en (em)	ahN	Similar to *on* with little emphasis on *n*. Now hold your nose, say *on*.
in (im), ain (aim)	aN	Similar to *an* with little emphasis on *n*
oin	waN	Similar to *wa* of *wag*
ien	yaN	Similar to *yan* of *Yankee*
on (om)	ohN	Similar to *on* as in *long*
un (um)	uhN	Similar to *un* as in *under*

Concentrate on Consonants

Most final consonants are not pronounced except for final *c*, *r*, *f*, and *l* (think of the word *careful*). Final *s* is not pronounced in French, so avoid the temptation. Doing so will quickly unveil your amateur status.

French Letter	Symbol	Pronunciation Guide
b, d, f, k, l, m, n, p, s, t, v, z	The same	Same as English
c (hard sound before a, o, u, or consonant) qu, final q	k	Say the *c* as in *card*.
c (soft sound before e, i, y), ç, s at beginning of word, s next to a consonant, -tion, x (only in the words given)	s	Say the *c* as in *cent*.
ch	sh	Say the *ch* as in *machine*.
g (hard sound before a, o, u, or consonant), gu (before i, e, y)	g	Say the *g* as in *good*.

French Letter	Symbol	Pronunciation Guide
g (soft sound before e, i, y), ge (soft before a, o), j	zh	Say the *s* as in plea*s*ure.
gn	ny	Say the *n* as in u*n*ion.
h		Always silent.

Most of the time, *h* is used as a vowel and, therefore, requires elision with a vowel that might precede it: *l'homme* (*the man*). In other instances, *h* is used as a consonant and does not require elision with the preceding vowel: *le héros*. To tell how *h* is being used, you must look in a dictionary, where the consonant *h* is usually indicated with an asterisk (*).

French Letter	Symbol	Pronunciation Guide
r	r	No equivalent

An Extra Workout

The French *r* requires the participation of your throat. First, drop your tongue to the bottom of your mouth and rest it against your teeth. Keep it out pressed there, out of your way. Now clear your throat or gargle and say "r" at the back of your throat at the same time. That's it—you've got the French *r*. A few words of advice: Do not roll your *r*; that's what they do in Spanish. Do not roll your tongue; that's what we do in English.

French Letter	Symbol	Pronunciation Guide
s (between vowels), *s*ion	z	Say *z* as in *z*ero.
th	t	Say *t* as in *t*o. There is no *th* sound in French.
x + consonant	ks	Say *xc* as in e*xc*el.
x + vowel	ehg	Say *ehg* as in egg.

Chapter 1

Strategies for Success

In This Chapter

- Starting out right
- The things you know
- Speaking idiomatically

So you've decided to learn French and you want to get off to a running start. Now you're looking for an uncomplicated but efficient way to accomplish this goal. It's simple: Just jump right in. That's right. Totally immerse yourself in anything and everything French. You have to have *une affaire d'amour* with the language, the culture, and the customs of the francophone world. If you want the key to a long-lasting, fulfilling, delightful relationship with French, just follow these tried and true suggestions:

- Examine your goals honestly. Assess your linguistic and auditory abilities. Decide how much time and energy you're willing to invest in your studies and then stick to your game plan. There's no hurry! Proceed at the pace that suits your needs.

- Make sure to invest in a good bilingual dictionary. Pocket varieties (which generally cost between $8 and $18) are more than sufficient for many learners. For the more serious-minded, however, a larger, more in-depth dictionary may prove necessary. Among the more popular, easy-to-use, comprehensive dictionaries, with a wide range of up-to-the-minute, colloquial, and idiomatic words and expressions are *Collins-Robert* (approximately $35) and *Larousse* (approximately $60).

- Never pass up an opportunity to become involved in the language. A wide variety of French films is available at large video stores (don't cheat and read the subtitles); public service radio and television broadcast many French programs; French magazines and newspapers are available in most major American cities. Look and listen all the time! Borrow language tapes from your local library or college and concentrate on the sounds of French.

- Read! Read! Read! Read everything you can get your hands on. Read to yourself, or out loud in front of a mirror, or to your good friends. It's easy to practice your comprehension and your accent all at once. Try comic books, children's books, and fairy tales. They're fun and entertaining! Pick up a copy of *Le Monde*, a French newspaper, and focus on what's happening in the francophone world.

- Find the most comfortable, learning-centered spot in your home and set up *un coin français* (a French corner). Use posters and articles to decorate this spot that will, from now on, be dedicated to your new project. Hang labeled pictures of vocabulary items you want to master. Organize and keep your French materials in this special area.

It's Time to Begin

Don't get nervous, but here's a quick pop quiz to see how much you know. Do you recognize: café, restaurant, amateur, boutique, bureau? Of course you do. Your knowledge of French is undoubtedly surprisingly extensive. You probably don't even realize just how many French words and expressions are already part of your vocabulary. And there are loads of phrases so similar to English that you will find them very easy to use and understand with a minimal amount of effort.

Creating with Cognates

Want to develop a rather extensive French vocabulary in no time flat? It's a piece of cake! Just learn those cognates! What's a cognate? Quite simply it's a word that is spelled exactly the same, or almost the same, as a word in English and that has the same meaning. Sometimes we've actually borrowed the word from French, letter for letter, and have made it a part of our own vocabulary. Sure, cognates are pronounced differently in each language, but the meaning of the French word is quite obvious to anyone who speaks English.

Tables 1.1 and 1.2 will help you get a jump start on your list. They provide lists of words that are the same (or almost the same) in both languages.

Table 1.1   Perfect Cognates

Adjectives	Nouns		
	Le	**La**	**L'**
blond	ballet	blouse	accident
blohN	*bah-leh*	*blooz*	*ahk-see-dahN*
certain	bureau	date	accord
sehr-taN	*bew-ro*	*daht*	*ah-kohr*
content	chef	dispute	ambulance
kohN-tahN	*shehf*	*dees-pewt*	*ahN-bew-lahNs*
immense	client	note	animal
ee-mahNs	*klee-yahN*	*noht*	*ah-nee-mahl*
permanent	sandwich	route	omelette
pehr-mah-nahN	*sahNd-weesh*	*root*	*ohm-leht*
possible	soda	table	orange
poh-seebl	*soh-dah*	*tahbl*	*oh-rahnzh*

Near Cognates

Table 1.2 lists the cognates that are nearly the same in both French and English. Take your time pronouncing the French words and compare them to their English equivalents. Remember: Your goal is to sound French.

Table 1.2   Almost Perfect Cognates

Adjectives	Nouns		
	Le	**La**	**L'**
américain *ah-may-ree-kaN*	bébé *bay-bay*	banque *bahNk*	acteur *ahk-tuhr*
amusant *ah-mew-zahN*	dictionnaire *deek-syoh-nehr*	couleur *koo-luhr*	adresse *ah-drehs*
bleu *bluh*	dîner *dee-nay*	famille *fah-mee-y*	âge *ahzh*
délicieux *day-lee-syuh*	papier *pah-pyay*	lampe *lahNp*	appartement *ah-pahr-tuh-mahN*
différent *dee-fay-rahN*	parc *pahrk*	musique *mew-zeek*	artiste *ahr-teest*
intéressant *aN-tay-reh-sahN*	téléphone *tay-lay-fohn*	pharmacie *fahr-mah-see*	hôtel *o-tehl*
populaire *poh-pew-lehr*	touriste *too-reest*	soupe *soop*	oncle *ohNkl*
riche *reesh*	vendeur *vahN-duhr*	télévision *tay-lay-vee-zyohN*	université *ew-nee-vehr-see-tay*

Verbs

Verbs (action words) can also be cognates. Most French verbs fall into one of three families: *-er* verbs, *-ir* verbs, and *-re* verbs. These verbs are considered regular because all verbs in the same family follow the same rules.

All French verbs must be conjugated. This means the verb form must have an ending that matches its subject. We do this automatically and naturally in

English without giving it a moment's thought. It's not that difficult in French and you will be able to learn it quickly. Verb conjugation will be explained in greater detail in Chapter 2.

Of course you'll find the verb cognates in Table 1.3 a snap to recognize.

Table 1.3   Verb Cognates

French	Pronunciation	French	Pronunciation
	The -er Family		
accompagner	*ah-kohN-pah-nyay*	passer	*pah-say*
aider	*eh-day*	payer	*peh-yay*
changer	*shahN-zhay*	préparer	*pray-pah-ray*
commencer	*koh-mahN-say*	présenter	*pray-zahN-tay*
décider	*day-see-day*	recommander	*ruh-koh-mahN-day*
demander	*duh-mahN-day*	refuser	*ruh-few-zay*
désirer	*day-zee-ray*	regarder	*ruh-gahr-day*
dîner	*dee-nay*	regretter	*ruh-greh-tay*
entrer	*ahN-tray*	réparer	*ray-pah-ray*
ignorer	*ee-nyoh-ray*	réserver	*ray-zehr-vay*
inviter	*aN-vee-tay*	signer	*see-nyay*
pardoner	*pahr-doh-nay*	tourner	*toor-nay*
The -ir Family		*The -re Family*	
accomplir	*ah-kohN-pleer*	défendre	*day-fahNdr*
applaudir	*ah-plo-deer*	répondre	*ray-pohNdr*
finir	*fee-neer*	vendre	*vahNdr*

Watch out for words that look like cognates but have a different meaning:

attendre (*ah-tahNdr*)	to wait
comment (*koh-mahN*)	how
la librairie (*lah lee-breh-ree*)	bookstore
rester (*rehs-tay*)	to remain
sale (*sahl*)	dirty
travailler (*trah-vah-yay*)	to work

Special Tricks

Some special tricks on pronunciation have already been mentioned. When you look at Table 1.4, you will see how adding an *s* after an accent circonflexe (ˆ) and how substituting an *s* for an *é* or adding one after it will help you figure out the meanings of many words.

Table 1.4   Special Tricks

Accent (ˆ)	English	é	English
coûter (*koo-tay*)	to cost	écarlate (*ay-kahr-laht*)	scarlet
croûte (*kroot*)	crust	échapper (*ay-shah-pay*)	to escape
fête (*feht*)	feast	école (*ay-kohl*)	school
forêt (*foh-reh*)	forest	épice (*ay-pees*)	spice
hôpital (*o-pee-tahl*)	hospital	éponge (*ay-pohNzh*)	sponge

Idiomatic French

What do we mean by an idiom? In any language, an *idiom* is a particular word or expression whose meaning cannot be readily understood by analyzing its traditional grammatical construction or its component words. Some common English idioms are:

> You'll have to pay through the nose.
>
> I have to buy some time.
>
> She called his bluff.
>
> Don't jump the gun.

All languages contain idiomatic expressions that must be memorized. That's why it's impossible to translate word for word from one language to another. A better idea is just try to think of the phrase you want in the language you want.

You will become better acquainted with many French idioms as you go from chapter to chapter.

An Extra Workout

Keep a file of index cards that contain the idioms you learn in each chapter. Try to use the ones that will be most useful to you in situations in which you will speak the language.

Chapter **2**

YOU Are the Subject

In This Chapter

- Hellos and goodbyes
- The verbs *être* and *avoir*
- Professions and countries
- Family members
- Possession
- Asking questions

A foolproof way to quickly immerse yourself in French is to find a foreign friend with a sympathetic ear. Then just jabber away. Talk about anything and everything that interests you. Don't worry about your mistakes. A real friend will politely let you get away with the less severe ones. Don't be shy about asking for help and corrections. No one is perfect. By all means use your dictionary or ask for help when you get stuck. Developing a friendship requires you to talk about yourself and to ask your new-found friend questions. Start to strike up a conversation by using the following phrases as an opener.

Since you don't know the person at all, a formal approach is *de rigueur* (mandatory). A typical opening conversation might start with many of these phrases:

French	Pronunciation	English
Bonjour	*bohN-zhoor*	Hello
Bonsoir	*bohN-swahr*	Good evening
monsieur	*muh-syuh*	Sir
madame	*mah-dahm*	Miss, Mrs.
mademoiselle	*mahd-mwah-zehl*	Miss
Je m'appelle	*zhuh mah-pehl*	My name is (I call myself)
Comment vous appelez-vous?	*kohN-mahN voo zah-play voo*	What is your name?
Comment allez-vous?	*kohN-mahN tah-lay voo*	How are you?
Très bien.	*treh byaN*	Very well.
Pas mal.	*pah mahl*	Not bad.
Comme ci comme ça.	*kohm see kohm sah*	So so.

I Am What I Am

If you're like most people, you like to talk about yourself and also find out about others. Making the other person the center of attention is sure to win you friends. To ask and answer the simplest questions in French, you need to know the verb *être* (to be). This is your first irregular verb, so be prepared to memorize all its forms as shown in Table 2.1.

Table 2.1 The Verb *être* (to be)

French	Pronunciation	English
je suis	*zhuh swee*	I am
tu es	*tew eh*	you are
il, elle, on est	*eel (ehl) (ohN) eh*	he, she, one is
nous sommes	*noo sohm*	we are
vous êtes	*voo zeht*	you are
ils, elles sont	*eel (ehl) sohN*	they are

If you detect an unfamiliar accent when speaking to an acquaintance, get ready to satisfy your curiosity by using *être* to ask about a person's origins.

Vous êtes d'où?   Je suis de … (city).
voo zeht doo   *zhuh swee duh*
Where are you from?   I am from … (city).

To express the state you come from, keep the following in mind:

- Use *de* (from) for all feminine states: any state ending in *e* and for any state whose name has an adjective:

    Je suis de Maine.
    Je suis de New York.

- Use *du* (from) for all masculine states: sates ending in any letter other than *e*:

    Je suis du Vermont.

- Use *des* (from) to say that you come from the United States:

    Je suis des Etats-Unis.

What's Your Line?

Use *être* to talk about your job or to ask about someone else's. The feminine forms are given in parentheses in Table 2.2.

Quel est votre métier?	*kehl eh vohtr may-tyay*	What is your profession?

Attention!

Remember that some occupations have only masculine or feminine forms despite the gender of the person employed. Other professions use the same word for masculine and feminine employees.

Table 2.2 Professions

English	French	Pronunciation
accountant	comptable	*kohN-tahbl*
dentist	dentiste *m.*	*dahN-teest*
doctor	docteur *m.*	*dohk-tuhr*
hairdresser	coiffeur (coiffeuse)	*kwah-fuhr (kwah-fuhz)*
jeweler	bijoutier (bijoutière)	*bee-zhoo-tyay (bee-zhoo-tyehr)*
lawyer	avocat(e)	*ah-voh-kah(t)*
manager	gérant(e)	*zhay-rahN(t)*
nurse	infirmier (infirmière)	*aN-feer-myay (ahN-feer-myehr)*
police officer	agent de police *m.*	*ah-zhahN duh poh-lees*
secretary	secrétaire *m./f.*	*seh-kray-tehr*

Where Are You From?

Curiosity naturally prods us into asking other travelers for their place of origin, especially if we detect a foreign accent. Faraway lands always seem so exotic and exciting, and people love to talk about their hometowns. Use *être* to express where you are from. Use Tables 2.3, 2.4, and 2.5 to find your place of origin. Note that all feminine countries end in –*e*.

Table 2.3   Feminine Countries

English	French	Pronunciation
Austria	l'Autriche	*lo-treesh*
China	la Chine	*lah sheen*
England	l'Angleterre	*lahN-gluh-tehr*
Germany	l'Allemagne	*lahl-mah-nyuh*
Greece	la Grèce	*lah grehs*
Italy	l'Italie	*lee-tah-lee*
Russia	la Russie	*lah rew-see*
Spain	l'Espagne	*lehs-pah-nyuh*

Table 2.4   Masculine Countries

English	French	Pronunciation
Canada	le Canada	*luh kah-nah-dah*
Israel	Israël	*eez-rah-ehl*
Japan	le Japon	*luh zhah-pohN*
Mexico	le Mexique	*luh mehk-seek*
United States	les Etats-Unis	*lay zay-tah-zew-nee*

If your travels take you far and wide you are probably fortunate enough to be able to plan a trip to another continent. The names of the seven continents appear in Table 2.5. Note that *L'Antarctique* (*lahN-tahrk-teek*/Antarctica) is the only continent that is masculine.

Table 2.5   The Continents

English	French	Pronunciation
Africa	l'Afrique	*lah-freek*
Antarctica	l'Antarctique	*lahN-tahrk-teek*
Asia	l'Asie	*lah-zee*
Australia	l'Australie	*loh-strah-lee*
Europe	l'Europe	*lew-rohp*
North America	l'Amérique du Nord	*lah-may-reek dew nohr*
South America	l'Amérique du Sud	*lah-may-reek dew sewd*

Going to Stay?

The preposition *en* is used to express that you are going *to* or staying *in* another country. Use *en* to express *to*, and also to express *in* before the names of feminine countries, continents, provinces, islands, and states and before masculine countries starting with a vowel:

> I am going to China.   I'm staying in Israel.
> Je vais en Chine.   Je reste en Israël.

Use the preposition *au* (*aux* for plurals) to express *to*, *in* before the names of some masculine countries, islands, provinces, and states that start with a consonant:

> I am going to Portugal. I am staying in the
> United States.
>
> Je vais au Portugal. Je reste aux Etats-Unis.

Coming

If you want to say that you are from (or that you are coming from) a country, use the preposition *de* to express *from* before the names of feminine countries, continents, provinces, islands, and states and before masculine countries starting with a vowel:

> I am from Belgium. I am from Israel.
>
> Je suis de Belgique. Je suis d'Israël.

The preposition *de* + the definite article (*le*, *l'*, *les*) is used to express *from* before masculine countries:

> I am from Japan. I am from the United
> States.
>
> Je suis du Japon. Je suis des Etats-Unis.

Near and Dear Ones

No introductory conversation is complete without a little bragging. How many times have you opened your wallet and started showing pictures of all your loved ones? It's almost second nature. Does it shock you to learn that many people actually enjoy seeing those corny pictures you carry with you? Use Table 2.6 to identify everyone correctly.

Table 2.6 Family Members

Male	French	Pronunciation
father	le père	*luh pehr*
grandfather	le grand-père	*luh grahN-pehr*
father-in-law	le beau-père	*luh bo-pehr*
child	l'enfant	*lahN-fahN*
brother	le frère	*luh frehr*
stepbrother	le demi-frère	*luh duh-mee-frehr*
stepson, son-in-law	le beau-fils	*luh bo-fees*
son	le fils	*luh fees*
uncle	l'oncle	*lohNkl*
cousin	le cousin	*luh koo-zaN*
nephew	le neveu	*luh nuh-vuh*
husband	le mari	*luh mah-ree*
son-in-law	le gendre	*luh zhahNdr*
boyfriend	le petit ami	*luh puh-tee tah-mee*

Female	French	Pronunciation
mother	la mère	*lah mehr*
grandmother	la grand-mère	*lah graN-mehr*
mother-in-law	la belle-mère	*lah behl-mehr*
child	l'enfant	*lahN-fahN*
sister	la soeur	*lah suhr*
stepsister	la demi-soeur	*lah duh-mee-suhr*
stepdaughter	la belle-fille	*lah behl-fee-y*
daughter	la fille	*lah fee-y*
aunt	la tante	*lah tahNt*

Female	French	Pronunciation
cousin	la cousine	*lah koo-zeen*
niece	la nièce	*lah nyehs*
wife	la femme	*lah fahm*
daughter-in-law	la belle-fille	*lah behl-fee-y*
girlfriend	la petite amie	*lah puh-tee tah-mee*

If the possessor is referred to not by name but by a common noun such as *the boy* or *the parents* (*He is the boy's father:* The father of the boy; or *That's the parents' car:* The car of the parents), then *de* contracts with the definite articles *le* and *les* to express *of the:*

de + le   du   C'est le père *du* garçon.

de + les   des   C'est la voiture *des* parents.

You Belong to Me

In English we use 's or s' to show possession after a noun. In French, however, there are no apostrophes to express possession. To translate "Marie's mother" into French, a speaker would have to say: "the mother of Marie," which is "la mère de Marie." The preposition *de* means *of* and is used to express possession or relationship.

Possessive Adjectives

The possessive adjectives *my*, *your*, *his*, *her*, and so on, can also be used to show possession as illustrated in Table 2.7.

Table 2.7 Possessive Adjectives

Used before masculine singular nouns or feminine singular nouns beginning with a vowel	Used before feminine singular nouns beginning with a consonant only	Used before all plural nouns
mon (*mohN*)/my	ma (*mah*)/my	mes (*may*)/my
ton (*tohN*)/your (fam.)	ta (*tah*)/your (fam.)	tes (*tay*)/your (fam.)
son (*sohN*)/his, her	sa (*sah*)/his, her	ses (*say*)/his, her
notre (*nohtr*)/our	notre (*nohtr*)/our	nos (*no*)/our
votre (*vohtr*)/your (pol.)	votre (*vohtr*)/your (pol.)	vos (*vo*)/your (pol.)
leur (*luhr*)/their	leur (*luhr*)/their	leurs (*luhr*)/their

Attention!

A possessive adjective must agree with the item possessed, not the possessor:

He loves *his* mother.	Il aime *sa mère.*
She loves *her* mother.	Elle aime *sa mère.*
He loves *his* father.	Il aime *son père.*
She loves *her* father.	Elle aime *son père.*

Son and *sa* both mean *his* or *her* because the possessive adjective agrees with the noun it modifies, not with the subject. Therefore, *her father = son père* because *son* agrees with the word *père*, which is masculine; and *his mother = sa mère* because *sa* agrees with the word *mère*, which is feminine.

What You Have

Perhaps you would like to discuss how many children you have or your age; or you might want to tell how you feel at a particular moment. The verb that you will find most helpful in these situations is *avoir* (to have). Like the verb *être* (to be), *avoir* is an irregular verb, and all of its forms (as seen in Table 2.8) must be memorized.

Table 2.8   The Verb *avoir* (to have)

French	Pronunciation	English
j'ai	*zhay*	I have
tu as	*tew ah*	you have
il, elle, on a	*eel, (ehl), (ohN) ah*	he, she, one has
nous avons	*noo zah-vohN*	we have
vous avez	*voo zah-vay*	you have
ils, elles ont	*eel, (ehlz) ohN*	they have

Asking Questions

If you don't want to seem too nosy and if your French is not as yet up to par, you'll probably be content to ask people simple yes or no questions. The four ways to do this are really quite easy.

Intonation

By far the easiest way to show that you're asking a question is to simply change your intonation by raising your voice at the end of the sentence.

Tu travailles aujourd'hui?
Are you working today?

An Extra Workout

I want to know all about you and my English is poor. Tell me as much as you can about yourself and your family in French. I'm very nosy, so don't leave out any details. Practice what you want to say until it flows smoothly.

N'est-ce pas?

You can also add the tag *n'est-ce pas* (*nehs pas*/isn't that so) at the end of the sentence:

Tu travailles aujourd'hui, n'est-ce pas?
You're working today, aren't you (isn't that so)?

Est-ce que

You may put *Est-ce que* (*ehs-kuh*) at the beginning of the sentence. Although it is not translated, *Est-ce que* does indicate that a question follows:

Est-ce que tu travailles aujourd'hui?

Inversion

Inversion, which is used far more frequently in writing than in conversation, means reversing the word order of the *subject pronoun* and the *conjugated verb form*. The rules governing inversion can get tricky, but don't despair. Use one of the other three methods mentioned if you want to make your life easy. You'll still be speaking perfectly correct French, you will be understood, and your question will be answered. If you are up to the challenge, here are the rules:

- Avoid inverting with *je*. It's awkward and is very rarely used.

- You can *only* invert subject pronouns with conjugated verbs. *Do not* invert with nouns!

- Tu travailles.   Travailles-tu?
  Vous parlez français.   Parlez-vous français?
  Elles habitent à Nice. Habitent-elles à Nice?

- With *il* and *elle* a -*t*- must be added to avoid having two vowels together. This generally occurs only with verbs in the -*er* family. The *il* and *elle* verb forms of -*ir* and -*re* verbs end in a consonant:

  Il travaille bien.   Travaille-**t**-il bien?
  Il choisit son dessert. Choisit-il son dessert?
  Elle répond vite.   Répond-elle vite?

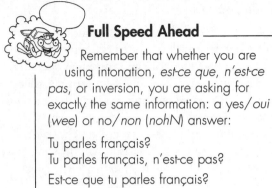

Full Speed Ahead

Remember that whether you are using intonation, *est-ce que*, *n'est-ce pas*, or inversion, you are asking for exactly the same information: a yes/*oui* (*wee*) or no/*non* (*nohN*) answer:

Tu parles français?
Tu parles français, n'est-ce pas?

Est-ce que tu parles français?
Parles-tu français?

How to Answer

If the answer is yes, use *oui* (*wee*) and then give your statement:

 Vous chantez?   Oui, je chante.

To answer yes to a negative question, use *si*.

 Tu ne chantes pas bien? Si, je chante bien.

If you want to say no, use *non* (*nohN*) and then add *ne* and *pas* (not), respectively, around the conjugated verb form. If there are two verbs, only the first is conjugated:

 Vous dansez?   Non, je ne danse pas.
         Non, je ne désire pas danser.

Put the following negative phrases around the conjugated verb if you want to vary your answers:

Ne … jamais (*nuh … zhah-meh*)	never
Je ne fume jamais.	I never smoke.
Ne … plus (*nuh … plew*)	no longer
Je ne fume plus.	I no longer smoke. (I don't smoke anymore.)
Ne … rien (*nuh … ryaN*)	nothing, anything
Je ne fume rien.	I don't smoke anything.

Asking for Information

Are you curious, like me? Then a simple yes-no answer never suffices. You want to get the complete picture, and for that, you'll need the facts. Use the questions in Table 2.9 to get the scoop.

Table 2.9   Information Questions

French	Pronunciation	English
à quelle heure	*ah kehl uhr*	at what time
à qui	*ah kee*	to whom
à quoi	*ah kwah*	to what
avec qui	*ah-vehk kee*	with whom
avec quoi	*ah-vehk kwah*	with what
de qui	*duh kee*	of, about, from whom
de quoi	*duh kwah*	of, about, from what
combien (de + noun)	*kohN-byaN (duh)*	how much, many
comment	*kohN-mahN*	how
où	*oo*	where
d'où	*doo*	from where
pourquoi	*poor-kwah*	why
quand	*kahN*	when

continues

Table 2.11   Information Questions   continued

French	Pronunciation	English
qui	*kee*	who, whom
que	*kuh*	what
qu'est-ce que	*kehs-kuh*	what

Attention!

Use *que* at the beginning of a sentence and *quoi* at the end of a sentence to ask *what*:

Qu'est-ce que tu fais?   Tu fais quoi?
What are you doing?

To ask for information:

- Use intonation.

  Vous parlez (Tu parles) **avec qui**?

- Use *est-ce que*.

  Avec qui est-ce que vous parlez (tu parles)?

- Use inversion.

  Avec qui voyagez-vous (voyages-tu)?

An Extra Workout

It's your turn to be nosy. Write down a list of questions you would like to ask me. I'm a very interesting person, and I have a large family.

Chapter 3

At the Airport

In This Chapter

- On the airplane and in the airport
- All about the verb *aller* (to go)
- Using *y*
- Giving and receiving directions
- What to say when you don't understand

Plane rides can be long and tedious, especially when you cross time zones. All too often there are minor inconveniences and delays. The scenarios are endless. For any number of reasons you might prefer a different seat or have some typical tourist questions for the flight crew. If you're lucky enough to be traveling on a foreign airline, you might want to use your knowledge of the language to help you get some tips and information. Use the terms in Table 3.1 to help you face any problem you might encounter.

Table 3.1   Inside the Plane

English	French	Pronunciation
aisle	le couloir	*luh kool-wahr*
to board, embark	embarquer	*ahN-bahr-kay*
crew	l'équipage *m.*	*lay-kee-pahzh*
to deplane	débarquer	*day-bahr-kay*
emergency exit	la sortie (l'issue) de secours	*lah sohr-tee (lee-sew) duh suh-koor*
gate	la porte	*lah pohrt*
landing	l'atterrissage	*lah-teh-ree-sahzh*
life vest	le gilet de sauvetage	*luh zhee-leh duh sohv-tahzh*
(non) smokers	(non) fumeurs	*(nohN) few-muhr*
row	le rang	*luh rahN*
seat	la place, le siège	*lah plahs, luh syehzh*
seatbelt	la ceinture de sécurité	*lah saN-tewr duh say-kew-ree-tay*
takeoff	le décollage	*luh day-koh-lahzh*

After You've Landed

Expect to find plenty of signs pointing you in all the necessary directions. In anticipation of the rather lengthy time it takes to unload your baggage, where should you proceed first? How about the bathroom? Do you need some foreign currency? Are you famished after the delicious culinary repast you received in flight? Table 3.2 provides all the words you need to know once you are inside the airport.

Table 3.2   Inside the Airport

English	French	Pronunciation
airline	la ligne aérienne	*lah lee-nyuh ahy-ryehn*
airplane	l'avion (m.)	*lah-vyohN*
airport	l'aéroport	*lahy-roh-pohr*
arrival	l'arrivée	*lah-ree-vay*
baggage claim area	la bande, les bagages *m.*	*lah bahnde, lay bah-gahzh*
bathrooms	les toilettes *f.*	*lay twah-leht*
bus stop	l'arrêt de bus	*lah-reh duh bews*
car rental	la location de voitures	*lah loh-kah-syohN duh vwah-tewr*
carry-on luggage	les bagages à main	*lay-bah-gahzh ah maN*
cart	le chariot	*luh shah-ryoh*
counter	le comptoir	*luh kohN-twahr*
departure	le départ	*luh day-pahr*
destination	la destination	*lah dehs-tee-nah-syohN*
elevators	les ascenseurs *m.*	*lay-zah-sahN-suhr*
entrance	l'entrée	*lahN-tray*
exit	la sortie	*lah-sohr-tee*
flight	le vol	*luh vohl*
gate	la porte	*lah pohrt*
information	les renseignements *m.*	*lay rahN-seh-nyuh-mahN*
lost and found	les objets trouvés	*lay zohb-zheh troo-vay*
to miss the flight	manquer (rater) le vol	*mahN-kay (rah-tay) luh vohl*
money exchange	le bureau de change	*luh bew-ro duh shahNzh*
passport control	le contrôle des passeports	*luh kohN-trohl day pahs-pohr*
porter	le porteur	*luh pohr-tuhr*
security check	le contrôle de sécurité	*luh kohN-trohl duh say-kew-ree-tay*
stop-over	l'escale	*lehs-kahl*

continues

Table 3.2   Inside the Airport   continued

English	French	Pronunciation
suitcase	la valise	*lah vah-leez*
taxis	les taxis	*lay tahk-see*
ticket	le billet, le ticket	*luh bee-yeh, luh tee-keh*
trip	le voyage	*luh vwah-yahzh*

Where Are You Going?

Getting lost in today's modern, sprawling international airports is rather easy. To find your way around, you'll need to know how to ask the right questions.

Où est le comptoir?
oo eh luh kohN-twahr
Where is the counter?

Le comptoir, s'il vous plaît.
luh kohN-twahr seel voo pleh
The counter, please.

Où sont les bagages?
oo sohN lay bah-gahzh
Where is the baggage claim?

Les bagages, s'il vous plaît.
lay bah-gahzh seel voo pleh
The baggage claim, please.

If the place you are trying to find is near you, expect to hear:

Voici le comptoir.
vwah-see luh kohN-twahr
Here is the counter.

Voilà le comptoir.
vwah-lah luh kohN-twahr
There is the counter.

One verb that will really come in handy is shown in Table 3.3. *Aller* (to go), is an irregular verb that must be memorized.

Table 3.3   The Verb *aller* (to go)

French	Pronunciation	English
je vais	*zhuh veh*	I go
tu vas	*tew vah*	you go
il, elle, on va	*eel, (ehl) (ohN) vah*	he, she, one goes
nous allons	*noo zah-lohN*	we go
vous allez	*voo zah-lay*	you go
ils, elles vont	*eel (ehl) vohN*	they go

The Pronoun *Y*

Y, a pronoun meaning *there*, generally replaces the preposition *à (au, a l', à la, aux)* or other prepositions of location: *chez*-at the house (business) of, *contre*-against, *dans*-in, *derrière*-behind, *devant*-in front of, *en*-in, *entre*-between, *sous*-under, *sur*-on, *vers*-toward. *Y* can also mean it or them, in it/them, to it/them, or on it/them.

> Tu vas à Rome.
> Tu *y* vas.
> You go there.

> Mon stylo est sur la table.
> Mon stylo *y* est.
> My pen is on it(there).

> Je réponds au téléphone.
> J'*y* réponds.
> I answer it.

Attention! _____

Never use *y* to refer to people. *Y* only refers to places, things, or ideas.

Complications

When where you want to get to is not within pointing distance, you'll need further directions. The verbs in Table 3.4 can help you get where you want to go or can help you aid someone else who is lost.

Table 3.4   Verbs Giving Directions

French	Pronunciation	English
aller	*ah-lay*	to go
continuer	*kohN-tee-new-ay*	to continue
descendre	*day-sahNdr*	to go down
marcher	*mahr-shay*	to walk
monter	*mohN-tay*	to go up
passer	*pah-say*	to pass
prendre	*prahNdr*	to take
tourner	*toor-nay*	to turn
traverser	*trah-vehr-say*	to cross

Use either *tu* (singular) or *vous* (plural) as the subject of your command. Since the subject of a command is always understood to be *you*, drop the *tu* or *vous* and use the correct verb form. For *-er* verbs only, drop the final *s* from the *tu* form in all commands.

Tourne à gauche.   Allez tout droit.
Turn to the left.   Go straight ahead.

Excuse Me. What Did You Say?

Suppose someone gives you directions, and you just don't understand? The person with whom you are speaking could be mumbling, speaking at a rapid-fire pace, have a strong regional accent, or use unfamiliar words. There's no cause for embarrassment. The phrases in Table 3.5 can be an invaluable aid if you need to have something repeated or if you need more information.

Table 3.5 When You Don't Understand

French	Pronunciation	English
Excusez (Excuse)-moi	*ehk-skew-zay (ehk-skewz) mwah*	Excuse me
Pardon	*pahr-dohN*	Pardon me
Je ne comprends pas	*zhuh nuh kohN-prahN pah*	I don't understand
Je ne vous (t') ai pas entendu.	*zhuh nuh voo zay (tay) pah zahN-tahN-dew*	I didn't hear you
Répétez (Répète), s'il vous (te) plaît	*ray-pay-tay (ray-peht) seel voo (tuh) pleh*	Please repeat it
Parlez (Parle) plus lentement.	*pahr-lay (pahrl) plew lahNt-mahN*	Speak more slowly
Qu'est-ce que vous avez (tu as) dit?	*kehs-kuh voo zah-vay (tew ah) dee*	What did you say?

Getting Wherever You're Going

In This Chapter

- Means of transportation
- Using *quel*
- Cardinal numbers
- Telling time

If you're traveling in a French-speaking country, you can take advantage of several different means of transportation to get to your destination. Ask yourself the following questions: Are you traveling light? In that case, you might want to mingle with people and take buses, subways, and trains. How tight is your budget and how much time do you have? If money is no object or if you're in a hurry, a taxi might be your best option. Do you enjoy seeing the countryside? If you're confident and are familiar with foreign traffic laws and street signs, you might just want to rent a car.

To say how you're getting there use the irregular verb *prendre* (see Table 4.1). *Prendre* has a tricky pronunciation: All singular forms end in a nasal sound, but the third person plural, *ils/elles*, is pronounced quite differently. The double *n*s eliminate the need for an initial nasal sound and give the first *e* a more open sound.

Table 4.1   The Verb *prendre* (to take)

English	French	Pronunciation
I take	je prends	*zhuh prahN*
you take	tu prends	*tew prahN*
he, she, one takes	il, elle, on prend	*eel (ehl) (ohN) prahN*
we take	nous prenons	*noo pruh-nohN*
you take	vous prenez	*voo pruh-nay*
they take	ils, elles prennent	*eel (ehl) prehn*

Now you're ready to say how you're getting there:

> I take ...
> Je prends ...
> *zhuh phraN*

English	French	Pronunciation
the boat	le bateau	*luh bah-to*
the bus	le bus (l'autobus)	*le bews (loh-toh-bews)*
the car	l'auto *f.*	*lo-to*
the car	la voiture	*lah vwah-tewr*
the subway	le métro	*luh may-tro*
taxi	le taxi	*le tahk-see*
train	le train	*luh traN*

Traveling by Bus

If it's Paris you're visiting, the R.A.T.P. (Régie Auto-
nome des Transports Parisiens) directs the user-
friendly bus and subway system. Green Parisian buses
post their route and destination on the outside, front
of the bus and their major stops on the bus's sides.
The route of each line is indicated on a sign at every
stop it makes. Free bus maps (*autobus Paris—Plan du
Réseau*) are readily available at tourist offices and
some métro booths. Since tickets may not be purchased aboard the bus, they must be bought ahead of
time at a métro station or *bureau de tabac* (tobacconist).

> Where is the nearest bus stop?
> Où est l'arrêt de bus le plus proche?
> *oo eh lah-reh duh bews luh plew prohsh*

> How much is the fare?
> Combien coûte un billet?
> *kohN-byaN koo tuhN bee-yeh*

Traveling by Subway

Even more efficient are the 13 numbered subway
lines, indicated by different colors on subway maps
distributed everywhere: at métro stops, hotels,
department stores, tourist offices. Each métro station
displays a *plan du quartier*, a detailed map of the sur-
rounding area. Transfers from one subway line to
another are free, and connections are indicated by
orange *correspondance* signs. You may transfer as
often as you like on one ticket, provided that you do
not exit to the street. Exits are clearly marked by
blue *sortie* signs.

Where is the nearest subway?
Où se trouve la station de métro la plus proche?
*oo suh troov lah stah-syohN duh may-tro lah
plew prohsh*

Where can I buy a ticket?
Où puis-je acheter un billet?
oo pweezh ahsh-tay uhN bee-yeh

How much is the fare?
Quel est le prix du trajet?
kehl eh luh pree dew trah-zheh

How many more stops are there?
Il reste combien d'arrêts?
eel rehst kohN-byaN dah-reh

What's the next station?
Quelle est la prochaine station?
kehl eh lah proh-shehn stah-syohN

Where can I find a subway map?
Où puis-je trouver un plan du métro?
oo pweezh troo-vay uhN plahN dew may-tro

Traveling by Taxi

Taxi drivers always give a flat rate from the airport (for other trips, it's metered) but charge extra for handling luggage and may refuse to accept more than three passengers.

Where is the nearest taxi stand?
Où est l'arrêt de taxi le plus proche?
oo eh lah-reh duh tahk-see luh plew prohsh

Would you please call me a cab?
Appelez-moi un taxi s'il vous plaît.
ah-play mwah uhN tahk-see seel voo pleh

I would like to go ...	How much is it to ...
Je voudrais aller ...	C'est combien pour aller à ...
zhuh voo-dreh zah-lay	*seh kohN-byaN poor ah-lay ah*

Stop here.	Wait for me.
Arrêtez-vous ici.	Attendez-moi.
ah-reh-tay voo zee-see	*ehs-pay-ray mwah*

Traveling by Train

If you're going farther afield, the R.A.T.P. also provides service on the R.E.R. (Réseau Express Régional), the local suburban train system. The S.N.C.F. (Société Nationale des Chemins de Fer) boasts trains that are the fastest in the world. The popular T.G.V. (train à grande vitesse), travels within the entire country, and links Paris to the rest of the cities in France. It has attained the world record of 260 kilometers (162 miles) an hour.

Where is the nearest train station?
Où est la gare la plus proche?
oo eh lah gahr lah plew prohsh

I would like ...
Je voudrais ...
zhuh voo-dreh ...

a first (second) class ticket.
un billet de première (deuxième) classe.
uhN bee-yeh duh pruh-myehr (duhz-yehm) klahs

a round-trip ticket.
un aller-retour.
uhN nah-lay ruh-toor

a (non) smoking compartment.
un compartiment (non) fumeurs.
uhN kohN-pahr-tee-mahN (nohN) few-muhr

Is it a local (express) (commuter train)?
Est-ce un local (un express) (un train de banlieue)?
ehs uhN loh-kahl (uhN nehks-prehs) (uhN traN duh bahN-lyuh)

From what platform does it leave?
De quel quai part-il?
duh kehl keh pahr-teel

Traveling by Car

Driving in Paris can be treacherous: The drivers are unpredictable, the traffic is congested, and there are *very* few parking spots. If you're daring, go to *une location de voitures* to rent a car. Always compare before you make a final choice. Don't be surprised when the price at the gas pump is almost double or more what you generally pay back home.

I would like to rent a ...
Je voudrais louer une (give make of car).
zhuh voo-dreh loo-ay ewn

I prefer automatic transmission.
Je préfère la transmission automatique.
zhuh pray-fehr lah trahNz-mee-syohN
o-toh-mah-teek

How much does it cost per day (per week)
(per kilometer)?
Quel est le tarif à la journée (à la semaine)
(au kilomètre)?
kehl eh luh tah-reef ah lah zhoor-nay (ah la
suh-mehn) (o kee-lo-mehtr)

How much is the insurance?
Quel est le montant de l'assurance?
kehl eh luh mohn-tahN duh lah-sew-rahNs

Is the gas included?
Le carburant est compris?
luh kahr-bew-rahN eh kohN-pree

Do you accept credit cards? Which ones?
Acceptez-vous des cartes de crédit? Lesquelles?
ahk-sehp-tay voo day kahrt duh kray-dee/lay-kehl

Do you fill it up with gas?
Vous faites le plein d'essence?
voo feht luh plaN deh-sahNs

The French word *feu* refers to a traffic light. Stop *au feu rouge* (at the red light) and go *au feu vert* (at the green light). Should a *gendarme* stop you for a traffic infraction, try using your foreign nationality as an excuse: *Mais, je suis américain(e)*. Sometimes a simple apology can work: *Pardon (Excusez-moi). Je le regrette.*

Attention!

If you decide to rent a car, open the trunk and make sure there's *un cric* (*uhN kreek*/a jack) and *un pneu de secours* (*uhN pnuh duh suh-koor*/a spare tire).

Note also that Europeans use the metric system to measure distance—1 mile is roughly 1.6 kilometers; and 1 kilometer is roughly 0.6 miles.

Heading in the Right Direction

Learn those road signs—some are not as obvious as you'd think. Familiarize yourself with the following signs before you venture out on your own:

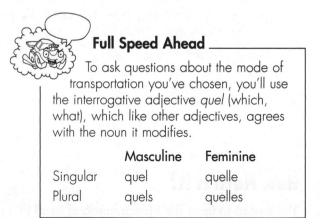

Full Speed Ahead

To ask questions about the mode of transportation you've chosen, you'll use the interrogative adjective *quel* (which, what), which like other adjectives, agrees with the noun it modifies.

	Masculine	Feminine
Singular	quel	quelle
Plural	quels	quelles

You also need to know your compass directions:

to the north	to the east	to the south	to the west
au nord	à l'est	au sud	à l'ouest
o nohr	*ah lehst*	*o sewd*	*ah lwehst*

How Much Is It?

You'll need to learn the French numbers listed in Table 4.2 to express which flight or bus you are taking or to figure out how much a rental car is going to cost you. You'll need these very same numbers when you want to tell time, count to 10, or reveal your age.

Table 4.2   Cardinal Numbers

French	Pronunciation	English
zéro	*zay-ro*	0
un	*uhN*	1
deux	*duh*	2
trois	*trwah*	3
quatre	*kahtr*	4
cinq	*saNk*	5
six	*sees*	6
sept	*seht*	7
huit	*weet*	8
neuf	*nuhf*	9
dix	*dees*	10
onze	*ohNz*	11
douze	*dooz*	12
treize	*trehz*	13
quatorze	*kah-tohrz*	14
quinze	*kaNz*	15
seize	*sehz*	16
dix-sept	*dee-seht*	17
dix-huit	*dee-zweet*	18
dix-neuf	*dee-znuhf*	19
vingt	*vaN*	20
vingt et un	*vaN tay uhN*	21
vingt-deux	*vaN-duh*	22
trente	*trahNt*	30
quarante	*kah-rahNt*	40
cinquante	*saN-kahNt*	50
soixante	*swah-sahNt*	60
soixante-dix	*swah-sahNt-dees*	70

French	Pronunciation	English
soixante et onze	*swah-sahNt ay ohNz*	71
soixante-douze	*swah-sahNt-dooz*	72
soixante-treize	*swah-sahNt-trehz*	73
soixante-quatorze	*swah-sahNt-kah-tohrz*	74
soixante-quinze	*swah-sahNt-kaNz*	75
soixante-seize	*swah-sahNt-sehz*	76
soixante-dix-sept	*swah-sahNt-dee-seht*	77
soixante-dix-huit	*swah-sahNt-dee-zweet*	78
soixante-dix-neuf	*swah-sahNt-dee-znuf*	79
quatre-vingts	*kahtr-vaN*	80
quatre-vingt-un	*kahtr-vaN-uhN*	81
quatre-vingt-deux	*kahtr-vaN-duh*	82
quatre-vingt-dix	*kahtr-vaN-dees*	90
quatre-vingt-onze	*kahtr-vaN-onze*	91
quatre-vingt-douze	*kahtr-vaN-dooz*	92
cent	*sahN*	100
cent un	*sahN uhN*	101
deux cents	*duh sahN*	200
deux cent un	*duh sahN uhN*	201
mille	*meel*	1000
deux mille	*duh meel*	2000
un million	*uhN meel-yohN*	1,000,000
deux millions	*duh meel-yohN*	2,000,000
un milliard	*uhN meel-yahr*	1,000,000,000
deux milliards	*duh meel-yahr*	2,000,000,000

Attention!

The French write the number 1 with a little hook on top. To distinguish a 1 from a 7, they put a line through the 7 when they write it: 7̸.

In numerals and decimals, where we use commas the French use periods and vice versa:

English	French
1,000	1.000
.25	0,25
$9.95	$9,95

French numbers are somewhat tricky until you get used to them. Look carefully at Table 4.2 and pay special attention to the following:

- The conjunction *et* (and) is used only for the numbers 21, 31, 41, 51, 61, and 71. Use a hyphen in all other compound numbers through 99.

- *Un* becomes *une* before a feminine noun:

  vingt et un garçons et vingt et une filles

- To form 71–79, use 60 + 11, 12, 13, and so on.

- To form 91–99, use 80 (4 × 20s) + 11, 12, 13, and so on.

- Do not use *un* (one) before *cent* and *mille*.

- *Mille* doesn't change in the plural.

Do You Have the Time?

Now that you have the hang of French numbers, it should be rather easy to express the time, as explained in Table 4.3.

What time is it?   At what time?
Quelle heure est-il?   A quelle heure?
kehl uhr eh-teel   *ah kehl uhr*

Table 4.3   Telling Time

French	Pronunciation	English
Il est une heure.	*eel eh tewn nuhr*	It is 1:00.
Il est deux heures cinq.	*eel eh duh zuhr saNk*	It is 2:05.
Il est trois heures dix.	*eel eh trwah zuhr dees*	It is 3:10.
Il est quatre heures et quart.	*eel eh kahtr uhr ay kahr*	It is 4:15.
Il est cinq heures vingt.	*eel eh saN kuhr vaN*	It is 5:20.
Il est six heures vingt-cinq	*eel eh see zuhr vaN-saNk*	It is 6:25.
Il est sept heures et demie.	*eel eh seh tuhr ay duh-mee*	It is 7:30.
Il est huit heures moins vingt-cinq.	*eel eh wee tuhr mwaN vaN-saNk*	It is 7:35.
Il est neuf heures moins vingt.	*eel eh nuh vuhr mwaN vaN*	It is 8:40.
Il est dix heures moins le quart.	*eel eh dee zuhr mwaN luh kahr*	It is 9:45.
Il est onze heures moins dix.	*eel eh ohN zuhr mwaN dees*	It is 10:50.
Il est midi moins cinq.	*eel eh mee-dee mwaN saNk*	It is 11:55.
Il est minuit.	*eel eh mee-nwee*	It is midnight.

When telling time be sure to do the following:

- Simply add the number of minutes to express the time after the hour; use *et* only with *quart* et *demi(e)*.

- Use *moins le* (before, less, minus) to express time before the hour.

- Use the following to express half past noon or midnight:

  Il est midi et demi.
  Il est minuit et demi.

- *Demie* is used to express half past with all other hours.

An Extra Workout

Look in your local newspaper and, in French, read aloud the movie times for the films you want to see.

Chapter **5**

Hotel Happiness

In This Chapter

- Getting the most from your hotel
- Ordinal numbers

A U.S. travel agent can help you find accommodations and make reservations that suit both your needs and your budget, no matter where you go in the French-speaking world. Should you have a spur of the moment change of plans, you can always go to a *Syndicat d'initiative* (*saN-dee-kah dee-nee-see-yah-teev*) or an *Office du Tourisme* to procure a room. You can expect to find the following types of lodgings in your travels:

- *Hôtels* are rated by The French National Tourist Office, which provides an official government guide granting ratings from 1 star (very modest) to 4 stars (deluxe). The accommodations and amenities the hotel offers, as well as its location determine the number of stars it receives.

- *Motels* are becoming increasingly popular in France. Expect to find them at the airport and near main roads in rural areas and outside large cities.

- *Pensions* are cozy, comfortable establishments that are usually family-run businesses. They provide anything from the bare minimum in services to the very luxurious. Their prices may include food and lodging. Staying in a pension is for the traveler who really wants to get to know the country by taking the path that's less traveled.

- *Auberges* are popular roadside inns, which generally provide services for people traveling by car. An *auberge de jeunesse* is a youth hostel which provides a dormitory setting.

- *Chambres d'hôte* are "bed-and-breakfasts" (usually in the proprietor's house) that are maintained by local families in small towns and villages.

- *Gîtes Ruraux* are private homes or apartments that are for rent.

It's always a good idea to check with your travel agency or the hotel's management before leaving home, to make sure all the amenities you require are available. Depending on your needs, you'll want to know the words for everything from bathroom to swimming pool. Be prepared for some surprises, even with reservations and assurances from your agent. Remember that it never hurts to ask questions when you are making arrangements or when you are in doubt. Note, too, that in French buildings the ground floor is called *le rez-de-chausée* (abbreviated *rez-de-ch*) and the basement is called *le sous-sol* (abbreviated *s-s*). The "first floor" is really on the second story of any building. See Table 5.1 for a basic list of hotel amenities.

Table 5.1   Hotel Facilities

English	French	Pronunciation
bar	le bar	*luh bahr*
bellman	le bagagiste	*luh bah-gah-zheest*
business center	le centre d'affaires	*luh sahNtr dah-fehr*
concierge (caretaker)	le (la) concierge	*luh (lah) kohN-syehrzh*
doorman	le portier	*luh pohr-tyay*
elevator	l'ascenseur *m.*	*lah-sahN-suhr*
fitness center	le club santé	*luh klewb sahN-tay*
gift shop	la boutique	*lah boo-teek*
maid service	la gouvernante	*lah goo-vehr-nahNt*
restaurant	le restaurant	*luh rehs-toh-rahN*
staircase	l'escalier *m.*	*lehs-kahl-yay*
swimming pool	la piscine	*lah pee-seen*
valet parking	l'attendance *f.* du garage	*lah-tahN-dahNs dew gah-rahzh*

Getting What You Want

Is something missing? Are you dissatisfied with your accommodations? If you need something to make your stay more enjoyable, don't be afraid to speak up. Table 5.2 lists a few items you might want or need:

I would like …	Je voudrais …	*zhuh voo-dreh*
I need …	Il me faut …	*eel muh foh*

I need …	J'ai besoin de (d')	*zhay buh zwaN duh*
Please send me …	Veuillez m'envoyer …	*vuh-yay mahN-vwah-yay*
There isn't (aren't) …	Il n'y a pas de …	*eel nyah pah duh*

Don't forget to show good manners by using the following phrases:

please	s'il vous plaît	*seel voo pleh*
thank you very much	merci beaucoup	*mehr-see bo-koo*
you're welcome	de rien	*duh ryaN*
you're welcome	pas de quoi	*pahd kwah*
don't mention it	Je vous en prie.	*zhuh voo zahN pree*

Table 5.2   Wants and Needs

English	French	Pronunciation
air conditioning	la climatisation	*lah klee-mah-tee-zah-syohN*
an ashtray	un cendrier	*uhN sahN-dree-yay*
a balcony	un balcon	*uhN bahl-kohN*
a bar of soap	une savonnette	*ewn sah-voh-neht*
a bathroom	une salle de bains	*ewn sahl duh baN*
a blanket	une couverture	*ewn koo-vehr-tewr*

English	French	Pronunciation
a hair dryer	un sèche-cheveux	*uhN sehsh shuh-vuh*
hangers	des cintres	*day saNtr*
a key	une clé (clef)	*ewn klay (klay)*
ice cubes	des glaçons	*deh glah-sohN*
some mineral water	de l'eau minérale	*duh lo mee-nay-rahl*
on the courtyard	côté cour	*koh-tay koor*
on the garden	côté jardin	*koh-tay zhahr-daN*
on the sea	côté mer	*koh-tay mehr*
a pillow	un oreiller	*uhN noh-reh-yay*
a safe (deposit box)	un coffre	*uhN kohfr*
a shower	une douche	*ewn doosh*
a single (double) room	une chambre à un (deux) lit(s)	*ewn shahNbr ah uhN (duh) lee*
a telephone	un téléphone	*uhN tay-lay-fohn*
a television (color)	une télévision (en couleurs)	*ewn tay-lay-vee-zyohN (ahN koo-luhr)*
tissues	des mouchoirs en papier	*day moo-shwahr ahN pah-pyay*
toilet paper	un rouleau de papier hygiénique	*uhN roo-lo duh pah-pyayee-zhyay-neek*
a towel	une serviette	*ewn sehr-vyeht*
a beach towel	un drap de bain	*uhN drah duh baN*
a transformer	un transformateur	*uhN trahNz-fohr-mah-tuhr*

Up, Up, and Away

I'd bet that like most of us, you've had an elevator experience—either in a hotel or elsewhere—in which you've felt like a large sardine in a small can. When you're pushed to the back or squished to the side, you have to hope that a kind and gentle soul will wiggle a hand free and ask: *Quel étage, s'il vous plaît (kehl ay-tahzh seel voo pleh)*? You will need the ordinal numbers in Table 5.3 to give a correct answer, such as: *Le troisième étage, s'il vous plaît (luh trwah-zyehm ay-tahzh seel voo pleh)*.

Table 5.3 Ordinal Numbers

French	Pronunciation	English
premier (première)	*pruh-myay (pruh-myehr)*	1st
deuxième (second[e])	*duh-zyehm (suh-gohN[d])*	2nd
troisième	*trwah-zyehm*	3rd
quatrième	*kah-tree-yehm*	4th
cinquième	*saN-kyehm*	5th
sixième	*see-zyehm*	6th
septième	*seh-tyehm*	7th
huitième	*wee-tyehm*	8th
neuvième	*nuh-vyehm*	9th
dixième	*dee-zyehm*	10th
onzième	*ohN-zyehm*	11th
douzième	*doo-zyehm*	12th
vingtième	*vaN-tyehm*	20th
vingt et un(e)ième	*vaN-tay-uhN (ewn)-nyehm*	21st
soixante-douzième	*swah-sahNt doo-zyehm*	72nd
centième	*sahN-tyehm*	100th

- The only ordinal numbers that must agree in gender (masculine or feminine) with the noun they describe are *premier* and *second*.

son premier roman — his (her) first novel
sa première chanson — his (her) first song

- Except for *premier* and *second*, add *-ième* to all cardinal numbers to form the ordinal number. Drop the silent *e* before *-ième*.

- Observe that *u* was added in *cinquième*, and *v* replaced *f* in *neuvième*.

- *Second(e)* is generally used in a series that does not go beyond two.

- Elision (the definite article *le* or *la* does not drop its vowel) does not occur with *huitième* and *onzième*.

  le huitième mois   the eighth month
  la onzième année   the eleventh year

Chapter **6**

What a Gorgeous Day!

In This Chapter

- Seasons and the weather
- The verb *faire*
- Days of the week
- Months of the year
- Remembering a date

Trips are taken all over the world year-round. No matter when that special time may fall, you should familiarize yourself with the weather conditions to expect, so that you can plan and pack properly. And after you arrive in a country, you'll want to be able to read or listen to the weather forecast (*la météo-lah may-tay-o*) so you can arrange your sightseeing trips and outings accordingly. The phrases in Table 6.1 will help you with the weather.

Table 6.1   Weather Expressions

French	Pronunciation	English
Quel temps fait-il?	*kehl tahN feh-teel*	What's the weather?
Il fait beau.	*eel feh bo*	It's beautiful.
Il fait chaud.	*eel feh sho*	It's hot.
Il fait du soleil.	*eel feh dew soh-lehy*	It's sunny.
Il fait mauvais.	*eel feh moh-veh*	It's nasty (bad).
Il fait froid.	*eel feh frwah*	It's cold.
Il fait frais.	*eel feh freh*	It's cool.
Il fait du vent.	*eel feh dew vahN*	It's windy.
Il fait des éclairs. *m.*	*eel feh day zay-klehr*	It's lightning.
Il fait du tonnerre.	*eel feh dew toh-nehr*	It's thundering.
Il y a du brouillard.	*eel yah dew broo-yahr*	It's foggy.
Il fait humide.	*eel feh tew-meed*	It's humid.
Il y a des nuages.	*eel yah day new-ahzh*	It's cloudy.
Le ciel est couvert.	*luh syehl eh koo-vehr*	It's overcast.
Il pleut.	*eel pluh*	It's raining.
Il pleut à verse.	*eel pluh ah vehrs*	It's pouring.
Il neige.	*eel nehzh*	It's snowing.
Il y a des rafales. *f.*	*eel yah day rah-fahl*	There are gusts of wind.
Il y a de la grêle.	*eel yah duh lah grehl*	There's hail.
Il y a des giboulées. *f.*	*eel yah day zhee-boo-lay*	There are sudden showers.

Just How Hot or Cold Is It?

You might get confused when you hear the temperature in a French-speaking country. That's because
they use the Celsius scale rather than the Fahrenheit
scale to which we are accustomed. This means that
when the concierge tells you it's 20 degrees (Celsius),
it's really a balmy 68 degrees Fahrenheit. To ask for
the temperature simply say:

Il fait quelle temperature?
eel feh kehl tahN-pay-rah-tewr
What's the temperature?

Now here are possible answers to your question:

Il fait moins dix.	Il fait zéro.	Il fait soixante.
eel feh mwaN dees	*eel feh zay-ro*	*eel feh swah-sahNt*
It's 10 below.	It's zero.	It's 60 degrees.

An Extra Workout

Look at the weather map in your daily newspaper. Give the weather and temperature in French for cities throughout the country.

The Verb *Faire*

When you speak about the weather, you need the verb *faire*. Shown in Table 6.2, *faire* means *to make* or *to do*, and is also often used to speak about household chores and about playing a sport (even though in this case it translates poorly into English).

Table 6.2   The Verb *faire* (to make, to do)

French	Pronunciation	English
je fais	*zhuh feh*	I make, do
tu fais	*tew feh*	you make, do
il, elle, on fait	*eel (ehl) (ohN) feh*	he, she, one makes, does

continues

Table 6.2 **The Verb *faire* (to make, to do)** continued

French	Pronunciation	English
nous faisons	*noo fuh-zohN*	we make, do
vous faites	*voo feht*	you make, do
ils, elles font	*eel (ehl) fohN*	they make, do

You must conjugate *faire* when you use it in context:

Tu fais un voyage?   Elles font une promenade.

Are you taking a trip?   They are taking a walk.

What Day Is It?

You're definitely more likely to forget the day of the week when you are very preoccupied or busy. It's extremely important to keep track of the day when you're traveling so you don't wind up at a tourist attraction you absolutely had to see on the day it's closed. Study the days of the week in Table 6.3 so you don't miss out on anything.

In French, only capitalize days of the week when they are at the beginning of a sentence. When used elsewhere, unlike in English, they are written with a lower-case first letter.

Samedi est un jour.   Saturday is a day.

Je vais au supermarché   I go to the super-
le samedi.   market on Saturdays.

To express *on* when talking about a certain day, the French use the indefinite article *le:*

Le mardi il va au centre commercial.
luh mahr-dee eel veh o sahNtr koh-mehr-syahl
On Tuesday(s) he goes to the mall.

Table 6.3 Days of the Week

English	French	Pronunciation
Monday	lundi	*luhN-dee*
Tuesday	mardi	*mahr-dee*
Wednesday	mercredi	*mehr-kruh-dee*
Thursday	jeudi	*zhuh-dee*
Friday	vendredi	*vahN-druh-dee*
Saturday	samedi	*sahm-dee*
Sunday	dimanche	*dee-mahNsh*

Unlike our calendars, French calendars start with Monday. Don't let this confuse you when you give a quick glance. You want to make sure that you get to that appointment on the right day.

My Favorite Month

As you eagerly peruse glossy vacation brochures, you'll probably be wondering about the best time to take your trip. Table 6.4 gives you the names of the months so you don't wind up in the wrong place at the wrong time.

Table 6.4 Months of the Year

English	French	Pronunciation
January	janvier	*zhahN-vee-yay*
February	février	*fay-vree-yay*

continues

Table 6.4 Months of the Year continued

English	French	Pronunciation
March	mars	*mahrs*
April	avril	*ah-vreel*
May	mai	*meh*
June	juin	*zhwaN*
July	juillet	*zhwee-eh*
August	août	*oo(t)*
September	septembre	*sehp-tahNbr*
October	octobre	*ohk-tohbr*
November	novembre	*noh-vahNbr*
December	décembre	*day-sahNbr*

Unless used at the beginning of a sentence, the names of all months should be written in lower-case.

> Janvier est un mois.   Je vais en France en janvier.
> January is a month.   I go to France in January.

To make it clear that something is expected to happen *in* a certain month, use the preposition *en*.

> We are going to Europe in September.
> Nous allons en Europe en septembre.

To Every Season Turn, Turn, Turn

Weather-wise, some seasons are better than others for traveling in certain countries. Make sure to plan your trip for when the weather will be great, so you don't have to worry about hurricanes, storms, or other adverse conditions. Table 6.5 provides the names of the seasons.

Table 6.5   The Seasons

English	French	Pronunciation
winter	l'hiver	*lee-vehr*
spring	le printemps	*luh praN-tahN*
summer	l'été	*lay-tay*
autumn, fall	l'automne	*lo-tohn*

The French use the preposition *en* for all the seasons to express *in*, except for spring, when *au* is used:

> Elle va à Paris en hiver (en été, en automne, **au** printemps).
> She's going to Paris in the winter (summer, fall, spring).

When's Our Date?

No doubt, when making travel plans and arrangements, you will often have to refer to and ask for dates. The following questions will help you get the information you need about the day and the date:

> What day is it (today)?
> Quel jour est-ce?   Quel jour sommes-nous?
> *kehl zhoor ehs*   *kehl zhoor sohm-noo*
>
> What is (today's) date?
> Quelle est la date (d'aujourd'hui)?
> *kehl eh lah daht (do-zhoor-dwee)*

And the answers to these questions are:

> Today is …
> C'est aujourd'hui + (day) date
> *seh toh-zhoor-dwee*

Today is ...
Aujourd'hui nous sommes + (day) date
oh-zhoor-dwee noo sohm

To express dates for appointments, travel plans, and meetings in French, follow these simple guidelines:

- Dates in French are expressed as follows:

  day of week + le (cardinal) number + month + year
  lundi le onze juillet dix-neuf cent quatre-vingt-dix-neuf

- Use *premier* to express the first of each month. Use cardinal numbers for all other days:

le premier juin	June 1st
le deux juin	June 2nd

- Just as in English, years are usually expressed in hundreds. When the word for *thousand* is written in dates only, *mil* is often used instead of *mille:*

1999	dix-neuf cent quatre-vingt neuf
	mil neuf cent quatre-vingt neuf
2003	deux mil trois

Notice how the date is written in French:

French	English
le 14 septembre 1947	September 14, 1947
14.9.47	9/14/47

Remember to reverse the month/day sequence used in English.

You'll need certain time-related words and expressions when you have to make plans and schedule your time wisely. When time is of the essence, keep the expressions in Table 6.6 in mind.

Table 6.6   Time Expressions

English	French	Pronunciation
ago	il y a …	*eel yah*
the day after tomorrow	après-demain	*ah-preh duh-maN*
the day before yesterday	avant-hier	*ah-vahN yehr*
a day	un jour	*uhN zhoor*
during	pendant …	*pahN-dahN*
from	dès …	*deh*
in	dans …	*dahN*
last	dernier (dernière)	*dehr-nyah (dehr-nyehr)*
last	passé(e)	*pah-say*
a month	un mois	*uhN mwah*
the next day	le lendemain	*luh lahN-duh-maN*
next	prochain(e)	*proh-shaN (proh-shehn)*
today	aujourd'hui	*oh-zhoor-dwee*
tomorrow	demain	*duh-maN*
a week from today	d'aujourd'hui en huit	*doh-zhoor-dwee ahN weet*
a week	une semaine	*ewn suh-mehn*
a year	un an	*uhN nahN*
a year	une année	*ewn ah-nay*
yesterday	hier	*yehr*

Use the definite article to express *on* with dates.

> Je pars le douze janvier.
> I'm leaving on January 12.

On the Town

In This Chapter

- Sights for tourists
- How to make suggestions and plans
- How to give your opinion

It's important to plan a logical itinerary for travel in a foreign country. Group by vicinity all the important tourist attractions you want to see for the day. You wouldn't want to waste precious vacation time running back and forth across the city. The key is to have a good game plan!

With all the opportunities available to you in the French-speaking countries around the world, you'll have to decide on a daily basis if you're in the mood for sight-seeing or relaxing. Does your body scream for a leisurely pace or are you raring to pack your day with as many activities as possible? The brochures that are available at airports and tourist offices will suggest many interesting and exciting things to do. Table 7.1 provides the words and phrases you need to talk about your choices.

I would like to go …
Je voudrais aller …
zhuh voo-dreh zah-lay

Table 7.1 Places to Go

English	French	Pronunciation
to the amusement park	au parc d'attractions	*o pahrk dah-trahk-syohN*
to the aquarium	à l'aquarium	*a lah-kwah-ryuhm*
to the carnival	au carnaval	*o kahr-nah-vahl*
to the castle	au château	*o shah-to*
to the cathedral	à la cathédrale	*ah lah kah-tay-drahl*
to the church	à l'église	*ah lay gleez*
to the circus	au cirque	*o seerk*
to the flea market	au marché aux puces	*o mahr-shay-o pews*
to the fountain	à la fontaine	*ah lah fohN-tehn*
to the garden	au jardin	*o zhahr-daN*
to the museum	au musée	*o mew-zay*
to the nightclub	au cabaret	*o kah-bah-reh*
to the public square	à la place	*ah lah plahs*
to the zoo	au zoo	*o zo*

Seeing the Sights

Whether you decide to go it alone or opt to take a tour, the following phrases will come in handy:

Where is the tourist office?
Où est l'office du tourisme?
oo eh loh-fees dew too-ree-muh

What is there to see?
Qu'est-ce qu'il y a à voir?
kehs-keel yah ah vwahr

Where can I buy a map (a guide book)?
Où puis-je acheter une carte (un guide)?
oo pweezh ahsh-tay ewn kahrt (uhN geed)

At what time does it open (close)?
À quelle heure ouvre (ferme)-t-il?
ah kehl uhr oov-ruh (fehrm) teel

What's the admission price?
Quel est le tarif?
kehl eh luh tah-reef

Can children enter free?
L'entrée est gratuite pour les enfants?
lahN-tray eh grah-twee poor lay zahN-fahN

Until what age?	How much do they pay?
Jusqu'à quel âge?	Ils paient combien?
zhews-kah kehl ahzh	*eel peh kohN-byaN*

Is it all right to take pictures?
On peut faire des photos?
ohN put fehr day foh-to

I need a guide who speaks English.
Il me faut un guide qui parle anglais.
eel muh fo tuhN geed kee pahrl ahN-gleh

How much does he charge?
Combien prend-il?
kohN-byaN prahN-teel

Where are there trips?
Où y a-t-il des visites guidées?
oo ee yah-teel day vee-zeet gee-day

To express what you would like to see or are going to see, you will need the irregular verb *voir* (to see) shown in Table 7.2.

Table 7.2   The Verb *voir* (to see)

French	Pronunciation	English
je vois	*zhuh vwah*	I see
tu vois	*tew vwah*	you see
il, elle, on voit	*eel, (ehl) (ohN) vwah*	he, she, one sees
nous voyons	*noo vwah-yohN*	we see
vous voyez	*voo vwah-yay*	you see
ils, elles voient	*eel (ehl) vwah*	they see

May I Suggest

It's been your dream to see the Folies Bergères. Fascinating ads, posters, films, and pictures have enticed you and have piqued your curiosity. You don't know, however, how the others in your group feel about accompanying you. Go for it! Make the suggestion. There are two options in French that you'll find quite simple.

● You may use the pronoun *on* + the conjugated form of the verb that explains what it is you want to do:

   On va aux Folies Bergères?
   ohN vah o foh-lee behr-zhehr
   How about going to the Folies Bergères?

● Another way to propose an activity is to use the command form that has *nous* as its understood subject:

Allons aux Folies Bergères!
ah-lohN zo foh-lee behr-zhehr
Let's go to the Folies Bergères!

When using this command form, it is unnecessary to use the subject pronoun *nous*.

Full Speed Ahead

With *on* use the third person singular form (*il*) of the verb.

- Try telling a friend what you'd like to do and then ask for his or her feelings about the idea.

  I'd like to go the the Folies Bergères. What do you think?

  Je voudrais aller aux Folies Bergères. Qu'en penses-tu?
  zhuh voo-dreh-zah-lay o foh-lee behr-zhehr kahN pahNs-tew

An Extra Workout

The weather is delightful and you're eager to go out and have a great time. Suggest five things that we can do together and express each suggestion in two different ways.

Colloquially Speaking

At this point, you should be feeling rather confident about using French, so it's time to take a more sophisticated approach. There are a number of phrases you can use, all of which are followed by the infinitive of the verb (the familiar forms [tu] are in parentheses):

Ça vous (te) dit de ...	*sah voo (tuh) dee duh*	Do you want to ...
Ça vous (t')intéresse de ...	*sah voo zaN (taN)-tay-rehs duh*	Are you interested in ...
Ça vous (te) plairait de ...	*sah voo (tuh) pleh-reh duh* ...	Would it please you to ...
Vous voulez ... (Tu veux ...)	*voo voo-lay (tew vuh)*	Do you want to ...

Any of the phrases listed above can be made negative by using *ne* ... *pas*:

Ça *ne* te dit *pas* de (d') ...   jouer au tennis?
(Don't you want to ...?)

Ça *ne* vous intéresse   aller au musée?
pas de (d') ...
(Aren't you interested in ...?)

Do you know any grouchy-from-lack-of-sleep young adults who give rapid-fire yes or no answers to questions? As for the rest of us, we usually say "yes, but ..." or "no, because ...." In French, if you'd like to elaborate on your answer, here's what you'll have to do: Change the pronoun *vous* or *te* (*t'*) from the question to *me* (*m'*) in your answer.

Oui (Si), ça m'intéresse de (d') …	aller au musée.
Oui (Si), ça me plairait de (d') …	jouer au tennis.
Non, ça ne me dit pas de (d') …	aller au musée.
Non, je ne veux pas …	jouer au tennis.

So What Do You Think?

When you want to express a positive feeling about a suggestion that was made to you, you would say:

J'aime l'art moderne. J'adore la musique.
zhehm lahr moh-dehrn *zhah-dohr lah mew-zeek*
I like modern art. I love music.

Je suis fana de football.
zhuh swee fah-nah duh foot-bohl
I'm crazy about soccer. (I'm a soccer freak.)

If you have the occasion to do something or go somewhere new, different, exotic, out of the ordinary, you're certainly going to have an opinion about whether you liked it or not. Is it fun? Are you having a good time? Are you amused? Give your positive opinion by saying *C'est* (meaning "it is") + an adjective:

C'est ...	seh ...	It's ...
chouette!	*shoo-eht*	great!
extra!	*ehks-trah*	exraordinary!
formidable!	*fohr-mee-dahbl*	great!
génial!	*zhay-nyahl*	fantastic!
magnifique!	*mah-nyee-feek*	magnificent!
merveilleux!	*mehr-veh-yuh*	marvelous!
sensationnel!	*sahN-sah-syoh-nehl*	sensational!
super!	*sew-pehr*	super!
superbe!	*sew-pehrb*	superb!

Maybe the suggestion presented to you is unappealing. Perhaps you find the activity boring. To express your dislikes you might say:

Je n'aime pas l'opéra.	I don't like the opera.
Je déteste le ballet.	I hate the ballet.
Je ne suis pas fana de golf.	I'm not crazy about golf.

You wanted to be a good sport, so you tried the activity anyway. It was just as you thought: not your cup of tea. To give your negative opinion about an activity you can use *C'est* + an adjective:

C'est ...	seh ...	It's ...
affreux	*tah-fruh*	frightful, horrible
dégoûtant	*day-goo-tahN*	disgusting

désagréable	*day-zah-gray-ahbl*	unpleasant
embêtant	*tahN-beh-tahN*	boring
ennuyeux	*tahN-nwee-yuh*	boring
horrible	*toh-reebl*	horrible
la barbe	*lah bahrb*	boring
ridicule	*ree-dee-kewl*	ridiculous

Chapter 8

The Shopping Experience

In This Chapter

- Stores and what they sell
- Clothing: colors, sizes, materials, and designs
- Object pronouns
- Preferences
- Expressing your opinion

Do you agonize over what to buy that special some-one? Do you place great importance on selecting the perfect gift? Do you have endless debates with yourself over color, size, material, and design? Or do you choose the first item that strikes your fancy? Are you always in search of a bargain? How impor-tant to you is comparison shopping? Shopping doesn't have to be a chore. With a good plan of action, it can be a pleasant and enjoyable experience for even the most crotchety among us.

You can browse in a small boutique or have the extensive selection provided by a large, elegant mall (*un centre commercial/uhN sahNtr koh-mehr-syahl*) such as le Forum des Halles in Paris or the underground

Place Bonaventure in Montréal. Table 8.1 points you in the direction of stores that might interest you and the merchandise you can purchase in them.

Table 8.1 Stores (*Les Magasins/* lay mah-gah-zaN)

Store	French	Pronunciation
bookstore	la librairie	*lah lee-breh-ree*
department store	le grand magasin	*luh grahN mah-gah-zaN*
florist	le magasin de fleuriste	*luh mah-gah-saN duh fluh-reest*
jewelry store	la bijouterie	*lah bee-zhoo-tree*
leather goods store	la maroquinerie	*lah mah-roh-kaN-ree*
newsstand	le kiosk à journaux	*luh kee-ohsk ah zhoor-noh*
perfume store	la parfumerie	*lah par-fewm-ree*
record store	le magasin de disques	*luh mah-gah-zaN duh deesk*
souvenir shop	le magasin de souvenirs	*luh mah-gah-zaN duh soo-vuh-neer*
tobacconist	le bureau de tabac	*luh bew-ro duh tah-bah*

Remember to save your receipts when you make purchases in any foreign country. Foreign visitors are charged a value-added tax (TVA—*taxe à la valeur ajoutée*) on certain purchases. (This tax is often 13 percent on a minimum purchase of 2,000 euros.) Some countries will return this tax (which could be considerable) upon presentation of a sales slip. Go to the specially marked windows at the airport or in large department stores to see whether any money is owed to you. Keep in mind that you might also have to pay U.S. taxes on your purchases.

General Questions

Here are some general question that should help
you on your shopping spree:

Could you please help me?
Pourriez-vous m'aider, s'il vous plaît?
poor-yay voo meh-day seel voo pleh

Would you please show me …?
Veuillez me montrer …?
vuh-yay muh mohN-tray

Are there any sales?	Where can I find …?
Y a-t-il des soldes?	Où puis-je trouver …?
ee ah-teel day sohld	*oo pweezh troo-vay*
Are there any discounts?	Do you sell …?
Y a-t-il des rabais?	Vendez-vous …?
ee ah-teel day rah-beh	*vahN-day voo*

Where is (are) …?
Où est-ce qu'il y a …?
oo ehs-keel yah

Do you have something …?
Avez-vous quelque chose …?
ah-vay voo kehl-kuh shohz

English	French	Pronunciation
else	d'autre	*do-truh*
larger	de plus grand	*duh plew grahN*
smaller	de plus petit	*duh plew puh-tee*
longer	de plus long	*duh plew lohN*
shorter	de plus court	*duh plew koor*
less expensive	de moins cher	*duh mwaN shehr*
more expensive	de plus cher	*duh plew shehr*
better	de meilleure qualité	*duh meh-yuhr kah-lee-tay*

Clothing

You simply can't take a trip to France, the fashion capital of the world, without coming home with at least one article of clothing sporting a French label. It is really *de rigueur* (*duh ree-guhr*) to be *dans le vent* (*dahN luh vahN*/in fashion). Table 8.2 will help you in your quest for something *au courant* (*o koo-rahN/* in style).

Table 8.2 Clothing (*Les Vêtements/* lay veht-mahN)

Item of Clothing	French	Pronunciation
bathing suit	le maillot	*luh mah-yo*
belt	la ceinture	*lah saN-tewr*
blouse	le chemisier, la blouse	*luh shuh-meez-yay, lah blooz*
boots	les bottes *f.*	*lay boht*
brassière	le soutien-gorge	*luh soo-tyaN gohrzh*
coat (sport)	la veste	*lah vehst*
dress	la robe	*lah rohb*
gloves	les gants *m.*	*lay gahN*
hat	le chapeau	*luh shah-po*
jacket	la veste	*lah vehst*
jeans	le jean	*luh zheen*
jogging suit	le jogging	*luh zhoh-geeng*
negligee	le peignoir	*luh peh-nywahr*
overcoat	le manteau	*luh mahN-to*
pajamas	le pyjama	*luh pee-zhah-mah*
panties	la culotte	*lah kew-loht*
pants	le pantalon	*luh pahN-tah-lohN*
pantyhose (tights)	le collant	*luh koh-lahN*
pocketbook	le sac (à main)	*luh sahk (ah maN)*
raincoat	l'imperméable *m.*	*laN-pehr-may-ahbl*
robe	la robe de chambre	*lah rohb duh shahNbr*

Item of Clothing	French	Pronunciation
sandals	les sandales *f.*	*lay sahN-dahl*
scarf	l'écharpe *f.*,	*lay-shahrp,*
	le foulard	*luh foo-lahr*
shirt	la chemise	*lah shuh-meez*
shoes	les chaussures *f.*,	*lay sho-sewr,*
	les souliers *m.*	*lay sool-lyay*
skirt	la jupe	*lah zhewp*
slip (half),	le jupon,	*luh zhew-pohN,*
(full)	la combinaison	*lah kohN-bee-neh-zohN*
sneakers	les tennis	*lay tuh-nees*
socks	les chaussettes *f.*	*lay sho-seht*
stockings	les bas *m.*	*lay bah*
suit (for man)	le complet,	*luh kohN-pleh,*
	le costume	*luh kohs-tewm*
suit (for woman)	le tailleur	*luh tah-yuhr*
tie	la cravate	*lah krah-vaht*
umbrella	le parapluie	*luh pah-rah-plwee*
vest	le gilet	*luh zhee-leh*

Of course you want to make sure you wind up with items that fit right. Remember, too, that European and American sizes are quite different. A woman's size 10 dress in the United States would be a size 38 in France and a man's size 34 suit would be a size 44 in France. Start by telling the salesperson the following to arrive at your correct size:

I wear …	small	medium	large
Je porte du …	petit	moyen	grand
zhuh pohrt dew	*puh-tee*	*mwah-yaN*	*grahN*

For shoes you would say:

I wear shoe size …
Je chausse du … + size
zhuh shohs dew

Colors

Do you see the world in primary colors? Or do you tend to go for the more exotic, artistic shades? Table 8.3 will help you learn the basic colors so you can get by.

Table 8.3 Colors (*Les Couleurs*/lay koo-luhr)

Color	French	Color	French
black	noir(e) *(nwahr)*	blue	bleu(e) *(bluh)*
brown	brun(e) *(bruhN, brewn)*	gray	gris(e) *(gree[z])*
green	vert(e) *(vehr[t])*	orange	orange *(oh-rahNzh)*
pink	rose *(roz)*	purple	mauve *(mov)*
red	rouge *(roozh)*	white	blanc(he) *(blahN[sh])*
yellow	jaune *(zhon)*		

Attention!

Since colors are adjectives, they must agree with the noun they are describing:

un jupon blanc
a white half slip

une combinaison blanche
a white full-length slip

des jupons blancs
white half slips

des combinaisons blanches
white full-length slips

Full Speed Ahead

To describe a color as *light* add the word *clair*.

To describe a color as *dark* add the word *foncé*.

light blue   *bleu clair*
dark green   *vert foncé*

Materials

Did you even unpack only to wish you had brought along a travel iron? Or do you hang your wrinkled garments in a steamy, humid bathroom hoping for the best? Will you only go with permanent press or do you prefer richer materials that will give you a more worldly, sophisticated look? If you expect to make a clothing purchase while on vacation, Table 8.4 will help you select the material you prefer for your special wants and needs. Use the word *en* (*ahN*) to express "in."

Table 8.4   Materials (*Les Tissus*/lay tee-sew)

Material	French	Pronunciation
cashmere	en cachemire	*ahN kahsh-meer*
cotton	en coton	*ahN koh-tohN*
denim	en jean	*ahN zheen*
flannel	en flanelle	*ahN flah-nehl*
lace	en dentelle	*ahN dahN-tehl*
leather	en cuir	*ahN kweer*
linen	en lin	*ahN laN*

continues

Table 8.4   Materials (*Les Tissus*/lay tee-sew) continued

Material	French	Pronunciation
silk	en soie	*ahN swah*
suede	en daim	*ahN daN*
wool	en laine	*ahN lehn*

Designs

Suppose you're on the hunt for a chic sweater you saw in the latest fashion magazine. Or maybe you'd like a plaid pair of golf pants because you really want to stand out. Or perhaps you're not even into shopping, but you'd like to compliment someone on the good taste of his striped tie. Table 8.5 provides the words you need to describe patterns.

Table 8.5   Designs (*Le Dessins*/luh deh-saN)

Design	French	Pronunciation
in a solid color	uni(e)	*ew-nee*
with stripes	à rayures	*ah rah-yewr*
with polka dots	à pois	*ah pwah*
in plaid	en tartan	*ahN tahr-tahN*
in herringbone	à chevrons	*ah shuh-vrohN*
checked	à carreaux	*ah kah-ro*

Object Pronouns

Object pronouns replace direct and indirect object nouns to avoid the constant monotonous repetition of a word.

Direct objects (which can be nouns or pronouns) answer the question **whom** or **what** the subject is acting upon and may refer to people, places, things, or ideas.

Indirect objects answer the question *to* **whom** the subject is doing something or *for* **whom** the subject is acting. Indirect objects only refer to people.

Direct and indirect object nouns may be replaced by the pronouns in Table 8.6.

Table 8.6   Direct and Indirect Object Pronouns

Direct Object Pronouns			Indirect Object Pronouns		
me (m')	*muh*	me	me (m')	*muh*	(to) me
te (t')	*tuh*	you (familiar)	te (t')	*tuh*	(to) you (familiar)
le (l')	*luh*	he, it	lui	*lwee*	(to) him
la (l')	*lah*	her, it	lui	*lwee*	(to) her
nous	*noo*	us	nous	*noo*	(to) us
vous	*voo*	you (polite)	vous	*voo*	(to) you
les	*lay*	them	leur	*luhr*	(to) them

The French preposition *à (au, à la, à l', aux)* followed by the name of or reference to a person indicates that an indirect object is needed. Some verbs such as *répondre (à)*, *téléphoner (à)*, and *ressembler (à)* are always followed by *à* + person and will, therefore, always take an indirect object pronoun.

Object pronouns are placed before the verb to which their meaning is tied (usually the conjugated verb).

Il *la* prend.	Tu ne vas pas *lui* parler.
He takes it.	You aren't going to speak to him/her.

Full Speed Ahead

Read the following two sentences:

I write (to) her a post card.
I bought (for) him a car.

In English, *to* or *for* is often understood, but not used. So be careful in French when choosing a direct or indirect object pronoun.

Asking for What You Want

We've all had an experience with a salesperson hovering over us greedily anticipating making a huge sale. Don't they understand that sometimes we just want to browse? At other times, however, we have specific wants and needs and require assistance. Here are some phrases to help you deal with most common situations.

Questions a store employee might ask you:

Puis-je vous aider?	Vous désirez?
pweezh voo zeh-day	*voo day-zee-ray*
May I help you?	What would you like?

Just looking? Then you would answer:

> No, thank you, I am (just) looking.
> Non, merci, je regarde (tout simplement).
> *nohN mehr-see zhuh ruh-gahrd (too saN-pluh-mahN)*

If you want to see or buy something, you would answer:

> Yes, I would like to see … please.
> Oui, je voudrais voir … s'il vous plaît.
> *wee zhuh voo-dreh vwahr … seel voo pleh*

> I'm looking for …
> Je cherche …
> *zhuh shehrsh*

And of course, if you're a shopper like I am, you'd want to know:

Are there any sales?	Have you slashed your prices?
Y a-t-il des soldes?	Avez-vous cassé les prix?
ee yah teel day sohld	*ah-vay-voo kah-say lay pree*

Preferences

When the salesperson wants to help you make a choice expect to hear:

> Which shirt do you prefer?
> Quelle chemise est-ce que vous préférez?
> *kehl shuh-meez esh-kuh voo pray-fay-ray*

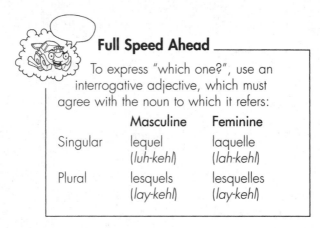

Full Speed Ahead

To express "which one?", use an interrogative adjective, which must agree with the noun to which it refers:

	Masculine	Feminine
Singular	lequel	laquelle
	(*luh-kehl*)	(*lah-kehl*)
Plural	lesquels	lesquelles
	(*lay-kehl*)	(*lay-kehl*)

Expressing Yourself

Girl, were you poured into those pants? That dress is you! What an adorable hat! To express your pleasure when you are satisfied with an item say one of the following:

I like it.	Ça me plaît.	*sah muh pleh*
It suits (fits) me.	Ça me va.	*sah muh vah*
It's nice.	C'est agréable.	*seh tah-gray-ahbl*
It's elegant.	C'est élégant(e).	*seh tay-lay-gahN*

If you're dissatisfied, you might use the following:

| I don't like it. | Ça ne me plaît pas. | *sah nuh muh pleh pah* |
| It doesn't suit (fit) me. | Ça ne me va pas. | *sah nuh muh vah pah* |

It's too small.	C'est trop petit(e).	*seh tro puh-tee(t)*
It's too tight.	C'est trop serré(e).	*seh tro suh-ray*
It's too short.	C'est trop court(e).	*seh tro koor(t)*
It's too long.	C'est trop long(ue).	*seh tro lohN(g)*
It's too loud.	C'est trop criard(e).	*seh tro kree-ahr*
It's too narrow.	C'est trop étroit(e).	*seh tro pay-trwaht*

If you're not satisfied and want something else:

I'm looking for something more (less) …
Je cherche quelque chose de plus (moins) +
adjective
zhuh shehrsh kehl-kuh shooz duh plew (mwaN)

Use a demonstrative adjective to express this, that, these, or those.

Used before masculine singular nouns beginning with a consonant	Used before masculine singular nouns beginning with a vowel	Used before all feminine nouns	Used before all plural nouns
ce (*suh*)	cet (*seht*)	cette (*seht*)	ces (*say*)
ce pantalon	cet imperméable	cette écharpe cette jupe	ces imper méables ces jupes

Demonstrative adjectives precede the nouns they modify and agree with them in number and gender. The special masculine form *cet* is used to prevent a clash of two vowel sounds together.

Food, Glorious Food

In This Chapter

- Buying food
- How to express quantity
- How to order in a restaurant
- How to get the dish you want
- Special diets
- The partitive and the pronoun *en*

Whether you make reservations in a swanky four-star restaurant or just stop by a local *charcuterie* (*shahr-kew-tree*/deli) to pick up a bite to tide you over, you need to know how to ask for the foods you want and how to refuse those that don't have any appeal. You'll also want to make sure you order the proper quantity. All your dietary cravings will be satisfied in this chapter.

Specialty Shops

First thing I do when I get to a foreign country is scout out the nearest food store, just in case I develop a severe case of the midnight munchies. In any French-speaking country you can enjoy the culinary delights that can be purchased in the shops listed in Table 9.1. Many of the names of the stores end in *-erie*. Drop this ending and add *-ier* (*-ière*) to get the name of the male (female) person who works in the store

Table 9.1 Food Shops

English	French	Pronunciation
bakery	une boulangerie	*ewn boo-lahNzh-ree*
butcher shop	une boucherie	*ewn boosh-ree*
candy store	une confiserie	*ewn kohN-feez-ree*
dairy store	une crémerie	*ewn kraym-ree*
delicatessen	une charcuterie	*ewn shahr-keww-tree*
fish store	une poissonnerie	*ewn pwah-sohn-ree*
fruit store	une fruiterie	*ewn frwee-tree*
grocery store	une épicerie	*ewn ay-pees-ree*
liquor store	un magasin de vins	*uhN mah-gah-zaN duh vaN*
pastry shop	une pâtisserie	*ewn pah-tees-ree*
supermarket	un supermarché	*uhN sew-pehr-mahr-shay*

Full Speed Ahead

It is very common to use the preposition *chez* (to [at] the house [business] of) + the person to express where you are going:

Je vais chez l'épicier (épicière).

Je vais chez le (la) boulanger (boulangère).

Food and More Food

Knowing the French names of the foods you like
and dislike will put you at a distinct advantage
whether you're in a store or at a restaurant. Use
Tables 9.2 through 9.9 to pick and choose at will.

Table 9.2   At the Grocery Store

Vegetables	Les Légumes	*lay lay-gewm*
asparagus	les asperges *f.*	*lay zahs-pehrzh*
beans (green)	les haricots *m.* (verts)	*lay ah-ree-koh (vehr)*
broccoli	le brocoli	*luh broh-koh-lee*
carrot	la carotte	*lah kah-roht*
cauliflower	le chou-fleur	*luh shoo-fluhr*
celery	le céleri	*luh sayl-ree*
cucumber	le concombre	*luh kohN-kohNbr*
corn	le maïs	*luh mah-ees*
eggplant	l'aubergine	*lo-behr-zheen*
lettuce	la laitue	*lah leh-tew*
mushroom	le champignon	*luh shahN-pee-nyohN*
onion	l'oignon	*loh-nyohN*
peas	les petits pois *m.*	*lay puh-tee pwah*
pepper	le piment, le poivron	*luh pee-mahN,* *luh pwah-vrohN*
potato	la pomme de terre	*lah pohm duh tehr*
rice	le riz	*luh ree*
spinach	les épinards *m.*	*lay zay-pee-nahr*
tomato	la tomate	*lah toh-maht*

Table 9.3 At the Fruit Store

Fruits	Les Fruits	*lay frwee*
apple	la pomme	*lah pohm*
apricot	l'abricot *m.*	*lah-bree-ko*
banana	la banane	*lah bah-nahn*
blueberry	la myrtille	*lah meer-tee-y*
cherry	la cerise	*lah suh-reez*
coconut	la noix de coco	*lah nwah duh koh-ko*
grape	le raisin	*luh reh-zaN*
grapefruit	le pamplemousse	*luh pahNpl-moos*
lemon	le citron	*luh see-trohN*
lime	le citron vert	*luh see-trohN vehr*
orange	l'orange *f.*	*loh-rahNzh*
peach	la pêche	*lah pehsh*
pear	la poire	*lah pwahr*
pineapple	l'ananas *m.*	*lah-nah-nah*
plum	la prune	*lah prewn*
prune	le pruneau	*luh prew-no*
raisin	le raisin sec	*luh reh-zaN sehk*
raspberry	la framboise	*lah frahN-bwahz*
strawberry	la fraise	*lah frehz*
tangerine	la mandarine	*lah mahN-dah-reen*
watermelon	la pastèque	*lah pahs-tehk*

Table 9.4 At the Butcher or Delicatessen

Meats	Les Viandes	*lay vyahNd*
beef	le boeuf	*luh buhf*
chopped meat	la viande hachée	*lah vyahNd ah-shay*
ham	le jambon	*luh zhahN-bohN*
lamb	l'agneau *m.*	*lah-nyo*
liver	le foie	*luh fwah*
pork	le porc	*luh pohr*
roast beef	le rosbif	*luh rohs-beef*

Meats	Les Viandes	*lay vyahNd*
sausage	les saucisses *f.*	*lay so-sees*
spareribs	les basses côtes *f.*	*lay bahs kot*
stew	le ragoût	*luh rah-goo*
tongue	la langue	*lah lahNg*
veal	le veau	*luh vo*

Fowl/Game	La Volaille/ Le Gibier	*lah voh-lahy/* *luh zhee-byay*
chicken	le poulet	*luh poo-leh*
duck	le canard	*luh kah-nard*
goose	l'oie *f.*	*lwah*
rabbit	le lapin	*luh lah-paN*
turkey	la dinde	*lah daNd*
venison	la venaison	*lah vuh-neh-zohN*

Table 9.5 At the Fish Store

Fish/Seafood	Le Poisson/Les Fruits de Mer	*luh pwah-sohN/lay* *frweed mehr*
bass	la perche	*lah pehrsh*
clam	la palourde	*lah pah-loord*
codfish	le cabillaud	*lah kah-bee-yo*
crab	le crabe	*luh krahb*
flounder	le carrelet	*luh kahr-leh*
frogs' legs	les cuisses de grenouille *f.*	*lay kwees duh gruh-* *nuhy*
grouper	le mérou	*luh may-roo*
halibut	le flétan	*luh flay-tahN*
herring	le hareng	*luh ah-rahN*
lobster	le homard	*luh oh-mahr*
mackerel	le maquereau	*luh mahk-roh*
monkfish	la lotte	*lah loht*

continues

Table 9.5   At the Fish Store   continued

Fish/Seafood	Le Poisson/Les Fruits de Mer	*luh pwah-sohN/lay frweed mehr*
mussel	la moule	*lah mool*
oyster	l'huître *f.*	*lwee-truh*
red snapper	la perche rouge	*lah pehrsh roozh*
salmon	le saumon	*luh so-mohN*
sardine	la sardine	*lah sahr-deen*
scallops	les coquilles	*lay koh-kee*
sea bass	le bar	*luh bahr*
shrimp	la crevette	*lah kruh-veht*
snail	l'escargot *m.*	*lehs-kahr-go*
sole	la sole	*lah sohl*
squid	le calmar	*luh kahl-mahr*
swordfish	l'espadon	*lehs-pah-dohN*
trout	la truite	*lah trweet*
tuna	le thon	*luh tohN*

Table 9.6   At the Dairy

Dairy Products	Produits Laitiers	*proh-dwee leh-tyeh*
butter	le beurre	*luh buhr*
cheese	le fromage	*luh froh-mahzh*
cream	la crème	*lah krehm*
eggs	des oeufs *m.*	*day zuh*
yogurt	le yaourt	*luh yah-oort*

Table 9.7   At the Bakery and Pastry Shop

Breads/Desserts	Pains/Desserts	*paN/duh-sehr*
apple turnover	le chausson aux pommes	*luh sho-sohN o pohm*
bread	le pain	*luh paN*

Breads/Desserts	Pains/Desserts	*paN/duh-sehr*
cake	le gâteau	*luh gah-to*
cookie	le biscuit	*luh bees-kwee*
cream puffs	les choux à la crème *m.*	*lay shoo ah lah krehm*
crescent roll	le croissant	*luh krwah-sahN*
danish	la danoise	*lah dah-nwahz*
doughnut	le beignet	*luh beh-nyeh*
French bread	la baguette	*lah bah-geht*
pie	la tarte	*lah tahrt*
roll	le petit pain	*luh puh-tee paN*

Table 9.8 At the Candy Store

Sweets	Les Sucreries	*lay sew-kreh-ree*
candy	les bonbons *m.*	*lay bohN-bohN*
chocolate	le chocolat	*luh shoh-koh-lah*

Table 9.9 At the Beverage Counter

Drinks	Les Boissons	*lay bwah-sohN*
beer	la bière	*lah byehr*
champagne	le champagne	*luh shahN-pah-nyuh*
coffee	le café	*luh kah-fay*
juice	le jus	*luh zhew*
lemonade	le citron pressé	*lun see-trohN preh-say*
milk	le lait	*luh leh*
mineral water	l'eau minérale *f.*	*lo mee-nay-rahl*
carbonated	gazeuse	*gah-zuhz*
non-carbonated	plate	*plaht*
tea	le thé	*luh tay*
wine	le vin	*luh vaN*

Getting the Right Amount

In France, the metric system is used for measuring quantities of food. Solids are measured in kilograms or fractions thereof, and liquids are measured in liters. Most of us are used to measuring in ounces, pounds, pints, quarts, and gallons. The following convenient conversion chart in Table 9.10 will help you get the hand of the metric system.

Table 9.10   Measuring Quantities of Food

Approximate Solid Measures

1 oz. = 28 grams	¾ lb. = 375 grams
¼ lb. = 125 grams	1.1 lb. = 500 grams
½ lb. = 250 grams	2.2 lb. = 1000 grams (1 kilogram)
1 oz. = 30 milliliters	16 oz. (1 pint) = 475 milliliters
32 oz. (1 quart) = 950 milliliters (approximately 1 liter)	1 gallon = 3.75 liters

The metric system is a complete mystery to me. So if, like me, you're a bit confused, Table 9.11 should make it even easier for you. Sometimes just asking for a box, bag, jar, and so on is easier. I suggest you memorize the amounts you're accustomed to: a pound, a quart, and so on.

Table 9.11   Getting the Right Amount

English	French	Pronunciation
a bag of	un sac de	*uhN sahk duh*
a bar of	une tablette de	*ewn tah-bleht duh*
a bottle of	une bouteille de	*ewn boo-tehy duh*
a box of	une boîte de	*ewn bwaht duh*

English	French	Pronunciation
a can of	une boîte de	*ewn bwaht duh*
a dozen	une douzaine de	*ewn doo-zehn duh*
a half pound of	deux cent cinquante grammes de	*duh sahN saN-kahNt grahm duh*
a jar of	un bocal de	*uhN boh-kahl duh*
a package of	un paquet de	*uhN pah-keh duh*
a piece of	un morceau de	*uhN mohr-so duh*
a pound of	un demi-kilo de	*uhN duh-mee kee-lo duh*
2 pounds of	un kilo de	*uhN kee-lo duh*
a quart of	un litre de	*uhN lee-truh duh*
a slice of	une tranche de	*ewn trahNsh duh*

All of these expressions of quantity include the word *de* (of). Before a vowel *de* becomes *d'*. In all other instances, *de* never changes:

beaucoup de bonbons	a lot of candies
une douzaine d'oeufs	a dozen eggs

You really want to sample that chocolate marquise your French cousin has prepared. You know the caloric content is high, but you long to savor its creamy, chocolately texture. Your cousin wants to give you more than "just a taste." Here are some expressions that will help you limit the amount you receive.

a little	un peu de	*uhN puh duh*
a lot of	beaucoup de	*bo-koo duh*
enough	assez de	*ah-say duh*
too much	trop de	*tro duh*

Making Purchases

Be prepared for the questions that you might be asked when shopping and the proper way to give a satisfactory answer:

What would you like?
Vous désirez?
voo day-zee-ray

May I help you?
Est-ce que je peux vous aider?
ehs-kuh zhuh puh voo zeh-day

Your answer might begin:

I would like …
Je voudrais …
zhuh voo-dreh

Could you give me …?
please
Pourriez-vous me donner …?
s'il vous plaît
poo-ryay voo muh doh-nay seel voo pleh

It's Mealtime

If you're going to eat in a restaurant, it might be necessary to reserve a table. When you call, make sure to include all the pertinent information, as follows:

I would like to reserve a table …
Je voudrais réserver une table …
zhuh voo-dreh ray-zehr-vay ewn tahbl

for this evening
pour ce soir
poor suh swahr

for tomorrow evening
pour demain soir
poor duh-maN swahr

for Saturday night
pour samedi soir
poor sahm-dee swahr

for two people
pour deux personnes
poor duh pehr-sohn

at 8:30 P.M.
à huit heures et demie
ah wee tuhr ay duh-mee

on the terrace, please
(outdoors)
sur (à) la terrasse,
s'il vous plaît.
*sewr (ah) lah teh-rahs seel
voo pleh*

There are a wide variety of eating establishments to accommodate your hunger and your pocketbook, whether you are going out for breakfast (*le petit déjeuner/luh puh-tee day-zhuh-nay*), lunch (*le déjeuner/ luh day-zhuh-nay*), dinner (*le dîner/luh dee-nay*), or an early afternoon snack (*le goûter/luh goo-tay*). If you're not in the mood for a formal restaurant, why not try:

une auberge	*ewn o-behrzh*	an inn
un bistro	*uhN bees-tro*	a small informal neighborhood pub or tavern
une brasserie	*ew brahs-ree*	a large café serving quick meals
une cabaret	*ewn kah-bah-reh*	a nightclub

un café	*uhN kah-fay*	a small neighbor-hood restaurant where residents socialize
un cafétéria	*uhN kah-fay-tay-ryah*	a self-service restaurant
une casse-croûte	*ewn kahs-kroot*	a restaurant serving sandwiches
une crêperie	*ewn krehp-ree*	a stand or restau-rant serving *crêpes* (filled pancakes)
un fast-food	*uhN fahst-food*	a fast food chain restaurant
un self	*uhN sehlf*	a self-service restaurant

You've been seated and you're ready to eat. But wait! Monsieur's place is missing something. Table 9.12 gives you the vocabulary you need when asking the waiter for cutlery, as well as other terms that will come in handy.

Table 9.12   A Table Setting

Table Setting	Le Couvert	*luh koo-vehr*
bowl	le bol	*luh bohl*
cup	la tasse	*lah tahss*
dinner plate	l'assiette *f.*	*lah-syeht*
fork	la fourchette	*lah foor-sheht*
glass	le verre	*luh vehr*
knife	le couteau	*luh koo-to*
menu	le menu, la carte	*luh muh-new, lah kahrt*
napkin	la serviette	*lah sehr-vyeht*

Table Setting	Le Couvert	*luh koo-vehr*
pepper shaker	la poivrière	*lah pwah-vree-yehr*
place setting	le couvert	*luh koo-vehr*
salt shaker	la salière	*lah sahl-yehr*
saucer	la soucoupe	*lah soo-koop*
soup dish	l'assiette à soupe *f.*	*lah-syeht ah soop*
soup spoon	la cuiller à soupe	*lah kwee-yehr ah soop*
tablecloth	la nappe	*lah nahp*
teaspoon	la cuiller	*lah kwee-yehr*
wine glass	le verre à vin	*luh vehr ah vaN*

What Do You Recommend?

Use the following questions and phrases for ordering both your drinks and your food:

What is today's specialty?
Quelle est la spécialité du jour?
kehl eh lah spay-see-yah-lee-tay dew zhoor

What is the house specialty?
Quelle est la spécialité de la maison?
kehl eh lah spay-see-yah-lee-tay duh lah meh-zohN

What do you recommend?
Qu'est-ce que vous recommandez?
kehs-kuh voo ruh-koh-mahN-day

I would like ...   I'll have ...
Je voudrais ...   Je prendrai ...
zhuh voo-dreh   *zhuh prahN-dray*

Please bring me ...
Apportez-moi, s'il vous plaît ...
ah-pohr-tay mwah seel voo pleh

I Need an Explanation

Are you confused and overwhelmed by the culinary terms on a French menu? The waiter will probably get lost in his explanation. Table 9.13 gives you the terms you need to know.

Table 9.13 What's on the Menu?

French	Pronunciation	Description
ailoli	*ah-yoh-lee*	mayonnaise flavored with garlic
à la bonne femme	*ah lah bohn fahm*	a white wine sauce with vegetables
béarnaise	*bay-ahr-nehz*	a butter-egg sauce flavored with wine, shallots, and tarragon
bercy	*behr-see*	a meat or fish sauce
blanquette	*blahN-keht*	creamy egg and white wine sauce usually served with stew
crécy	*kray-see*	carrots
daube	*dohb*	a stew, usually beef, with red wine, onions, and garlic
farci(e)	*fahr-see*	a stuffing
florentine	*floh-rahN-teen*	spinach
forestière	*foh-rehs-tyehr*	wild mushrooms
hollandaise	*oh-lahN-dehz*	an egg yolk, butter sauce with lemon juice or vinegar
jardinière	*zhahr-dee-nyehr*	vegetables
maître d'hôtel	*mehtr do-tehl*	a butter sauce with parsley and lemon juice
mornay	*mohr-nay*	a white sauce with cheese
parmentier	*pahr-mahN-tyay*	potatoes
périgourdine	*pay-ree-goor-deen*	mushrooms (truffles)
provençale	*proh-vahN-sahl*	a vegetable garnish
rémoulade	*ray-moo-lahd*	mayonnaise flavored with mustard

French	Pronunciation	Description
véronique	*vay-rohN-neek*	grapes
vol-au-vent	*vohl-o-vahN*	puff pastry with creamed meat

Table 9.14 will help you get from the appetizer through the main course. If you have any problems with the names of various types of meat or fish, refer back to Table 9.4.

Table 9.14   What Course?

French	Pronunciation	Description
Les Hors-d'oeuvres	*lay ohr-duhvr*	*Appetizer*
le tournedos	*luh toor-nuh-do*	small fillets of beef
crudités varíees	*krew-dee-tay vah-ryay*	sliced raw vegetables usually crudités varíees in a vinaigrette sauce
escargots à la bourguignonne	*ehs-kahr-go ah lah boor-gee-nyohn*	snails in garlic sauce
foie gras	*fwah grah*	fresh, sometimes uncooked goose liver, served with toasted French bread
pâté	*pah-tay*	pureed liver or other meat served in a loaf
quiche lorraine	*keesh loh-rehn*	egg custard tart served with meat (bacon or ham)
quenelles	*kuh-nehl*	dumplings
rillettes	*ree-yeht*	pork mixture served as a spread

French	Pronunciation	Description
Les Soupes	*lay soop*	*Soups*
la bisque	*lah beesk*	creamy soup made with crayfish
la bouillabaisse	*lah boo-yah-behs*	seafood stew
le consommé	*luh kohN-soh-may*	clear broth
la petite marmite	*lah puh-teet mahr-meet*	rich consommé served with vegetables and meat
le potage	*luh poh-tahzh*	thick soup made of pureed vegetables
la soupe à l'oignon	*lah soop ah loh-nyohN*	onion soup served with bread and cheese
le velouté	*luh vuh-loo-tay*	creamy soup
Les Viandes	*lay vyahnd*	*Meats*
le bifteck	*luh beef-tehk*	steak
le carré d'agneau	*luh kah-ray dah-nyo*	rack of lamb
le chateaubriand	*luh shah-to-bree-yahN*	a porterhouse steak
la côte de boeuf	*lah koht duh buhf*	prime rib
les côtes de porc *f.*	*lay koht duh pohr*	pork chops
les côtes de veau *f.*	*lay koht duh vo*	veal chops
l'entrecôte *f.*	*lahNtr-koht*	sirloin steak
l'escalope *f.*	*leh-skah-lohp*	scallopine, cutlet
le foie	*luh foie*	liver
le gigot d'agneau	*luh zhee-go dah-nyo*	leg of lamb
les médaillons de ... *m.*	*lay may-dah-yohN duh*	small rounds of ...
la poitrine de ...	*lah pwah-treen duh*	breast of ...
le pot-au-feu	*luh poh-to-fuh*	boiled beef
le rosbif	*luh rohs-beef*	roast beef
les saucisses *f.*	*lay so-sees*	sausages

Proper Preparation

Of course, you want to make sure your meal is cooked just the way you like it. The waiter may ask the following:

> How do you want it (them)?
> Vous le (la, les) voulez comment?
> *voo luh (lah, lay) voo-lay koh-mahN*

If you are very determined to have your meat pre-pared the way you like it, understand that French chefs have a different interpretation of the terms rare, medium, and well-done. Rare means almost alive, medium is a tiny bit more than our rare, and well done is a bit more than our medium. What the chef thinks is burned, is what we mean by well-done. He or she may prepare it well-done, but don't expect a smile when it is served. Table 9.15 will help you to express your wants and needs.

Table 9.15 How Would You Like It Prepared?

English	French	Pronunciation
	Meats and Vegetables	
baked	cuit au four	*kwee to foor*
broiled	rôti	*ro-tee*
boiled	bouilli	*boo-yee*
browned	gratiné	*grah-tee-nay*
breaded	au gratin	*o grah-taN*
chopped	hâché	*ah-shay*
fried	frit	*free*
sauteed	sauté	*so-tay*
grilled	grillé	*gree-yay*

English	French	Pronunciation
steamed	à la vapeur	*ah lah vah-puhr*
in its natural juices	au jus	*o zhew*
stewed	en cocotte	*ahN koh-koht*
mashed	en purée	*ahN pew-ray*
poached	poché	*poh-shay*
pureed	en purée	*ahN pew-ray*
roasted	rôti	*ro-tee*
very rare	bleu	*bluh*
rare	saignant	*seh-nyahN*
medium	à point	*ah pwaN*
well-done	bien cuit	*byaN kwee*
with sauce	en sauce	*ahN sos*
	Eggs	
fried	au plat	*o plah*
hard-boiled	durs	*dewr*
medium-boiled	mollets	*moh-leh*
poached	pochés	*poh-shay*
scrambled	brouillés	*broo-yay*
soft-boiled	à la coque	*ah lah kohk*
omelette	une omelette	*ewn nohm-leht*
plain omelette	une omelette nature	*ewn nohm-leht nah-tewr*

I Like It Spicy

Lots of herbs, spices, seasonings, and condiments are used to flavor French foods. Depend on menu descriptions or your server to help you determine whether the dish will be to your liking—bland or spicy. Table 9.16 will help you with the spices you might encounter.

Table 9.16   Herbs, Spices, and Condiments

Herbs, Spices, and Condiments	Les Herbes, Les Épices, et Les Condiments	lay zehrb, lay zay-pees, ay lay kohn-dee-mahn
basil	le basilic	luh bah-zee-leek
bay leaf	la feuille de laurier	lah fuhy duh loh-ryay
butter	le beurre	luh buhr
chives	la ciboulette	lah see-boo-leht
dill	l'aneth m.	lah-neht
garlic	l'ail m.	lahy
ginger	le gingembre	luh zhaN-zhahNbr
honey	le miel	luh myehl
horseradish	le raifort	luh reh-fohr
jam, jelly	la confiture	lah kohN-fee-tewr
ketchup	le ketchup	luh keht-chuhp
lemon	le citron	luh see-trohN
maple syrup	le sirop d'érable	luh see-roh day-rahbl
mayonnaise	la mayonnaise	lah mah-yoh-nehz
mint	la menthe	lah mahNt
mustard	la moutarde	lah moo-tahrd
oil	l'huile f.	lweel
oregano	l'origan m.	loh-ree-gahN
parsley	le persil	luh pehr-seel
pepper	le poivre	luh pwahvr
salt	le sel	luh sehl
sugar	le sucre	luh sewkr
tarragon	l'estragon m.	lehs-trah-gohN
vinegar	le vinaigre	luh vee-nehgr

Special Requests

Keep the following phrases handy if you have certain likes and dislikes, or dietary restrictions that you would like to make known:

I am on a diet.
Je suis au régime.
zhuh swee zo ray-zheem

I'm a vegetarian.
Je suis végétarien(ne).
zhuh swee vay-zhay-tah-ryaN (ryen)

I can't eat anything made with …
Je ne peux rien manger de cuisiné au (à la) …
zhuh nuh puh ryaN mahN-zhay duh kwee-zee-nay o (ah lah)

I can't have …
Je ne tolère …
zhuh nuh toh-lehr

any alcohol
aucun produit alcoolique
o-kuhN proh-dwee ahl-koh-leek

any dairy products
aucun produit laitier
o-kuhN proh-dwee leh-tyay

any saturated fats
aucune matière grasse animale
o-kewn mah-tyehr grahs ah-nee-mahl

any shellfish
aucun fruit de mer
o-kuhN frweed mehr

I'm looking for a dish …
Je cherche un plat …
zhuh shehrsh uhN plah

high in fiber
riche en fibre
reesh ahN feebr

low in cholesterol
léger en cholestérol
lay-zhay ahN koh-lehs-tay-rohl

low in fat	low in sodium
léger en matières grasses	léger en sodium
lay-zhay ahN mah-tyehr grahs	*lay-zhay ahN sohd-yuhm*

non-dairy	salt-free
non-laitier	sans sel
nohN-leh-tyay	*sahN sehl*

sugar-free	without artificial coloring
sans sucre	sans colorant
sahN sewkr	*sahN koh-loh-rahN*

without preservatives
sans conservateurs
sahN kohN-sehr-vah-tuhr

Back It Goes

At times the cooking or the table setting might not be up to your standards. Table 9.17 presents some problems you might encounter.

Table 9.17 Possible Problems

English	French	Pronunciation
… is cold	… est froid(e)	*eh frwah(d)*
… is too rare	… n'est pas assez cuit(e)	*neh pah zah-say kwee(t)*
… is over-cooked	… est trop cuit(e)	*eh tro kwee(t)*
… is tough	… est dur(e)	*eh dewr*
… is burned	… est brûlé(e)	*eh brew-lay*
… is too salty	… est trop salé(e)	*eh tro sah-lay*
… is too sweet	… est trop sucré(e)	*eh tro sew-kray*

continues

Table 9.17   Possible Problems   continued

English	French	Pronunciation
… is too spicy	… est trop épicé(e)	*eh tro ay-pee-say*
… is spoiled	… est tourné(e)	*eh toor-nay*
… is bitter	… est aigre	*eh tehgr*
… tastes like …	… a le goût de …	*ah luh goo duh*
… is dirty	… est sale	*eh sahl*

Fancy Endings

When it's time for dessert, choose from among the delightful specialties in Table 9.18 or from *des fromages variés* (*day froh-mahzh vah-ryay/cheeses*): *boursin, brie, camembert, chèvre, munster, port-salut,* and *roquefort.* When choosing a cheese you might want to ask:

Is it …?	Est-il …?	*eh-teel*
mild	maigre	*mehgr*
sharp	piquant	*pee-kahN*
hard	fermenté	*fehr-mahN-tay*
soft	à pâte molle	*ah paht mohl*

Finally, it's time for dessert, and there are so many French specialties from which to choose. Table 9.18 will help you make a decision.

Table 9.18   Divine Desserts

French	Pronunciation	English
une bavaroise	*ewn bah-vahr-wahz*	bavarian cream
des beignets	*day beh-nyeh*	fruit doughnuts

French	Pronunciation	English
une bombe	*ewn bohNb*	ice cream with many flavors
une charlotte	*ewn shahr-loht*	sponge cake and pudding
une crème caramel	*ewn krehm kah-rah-mehl*	egg custard served with caramel sauce
une gaufre	*ewn gohfr*	waffle
des oeufs à la neige	*day zuh ah lah nehzh*	meringues in a custard sauce
une omelette norvégienne	*ewn nohm-leht nohr-vay-zhyehn*	baked Alaska
des poires bellé Hélène	*day pwahr behl-ay-lehn*	poached pears with vanilla ice cream and chocolate sauce
des profiteroles	*day proh-fee-trohl*	cream puffs with chocolate sauce

Make sure you get the ice cream you want for dessert.

an ice cream	une glace	*ewn glahs*
a yogurt	un yaourt	*uhN yah-oort*
cone	un cornet	*uhN kohr-neh*
cup	une coupe	*ewn koop*
chocolate	au chocolat	*o shoh-koh-lah*
vanilla	à la vanille	*ah lah vah-nee-y*
strawberry	aux fraises	*o frehz*

Wine and Dine

The French usually drink wine with dinner. The wines you might order include the following:

| red wine | le vin rouge | *luh vaN roozh* |
| rosé wine | le vin rosé | *luh vaN ro-zay* |

white wine	le vin blanc	*luh vaN blahN*
sparkling wine	le vin mousseux	*luh vaN moo-suh*
champagne	le champagne	*luh shahN-pah-nyuh*

I Only Want a Taste

The partitive is used in French to express part of a whole, or an indefinite quantity and is equivalent to the English *some* or *any*.

Partitive	Used Before
du (de + le)	masculine singular nouns beginning with a consonant
de la	feminine singular nouns beginning with a consonant
de l'	any singular noun beginning with a vowel
des (de + les)	all plural nouns

Although *some* or *any* may be omitted in English, the partitive must always be used in French and must be repeated before each noun:

Bring me some mousse and some coffee, please.
Apportez-moi *de la* mousse et *du* café, s'il vous plaît.
ah-pohr-tay-mwah duh lah moos ay dew kah-fay seel voo pleh

In a negative sentence, or before an adjective preceding a plural noun, the partitive is expressed by *de* (no definite article is used).

> They don't have (any) fish.
> Ils n'ont pas *de* poisson.
> *eel nohN pah duh pwah-sohN*
>
> He prepares good desserts.
> Il prépare de bons desserts.
> *eel pray-pahr duh bohN duh-sehr*

The Pronoun en

The pronoun *en* refers to previously mentioned things or places. *En* usually replaces *de* + noun and may mean some or any (of it/them), of it/them, about it/them, from it/them, or from there:

> He wants some apples
> Il veut *des pommes*.
> He wants some of them.
> Il *en* veut.

> I don't want any meat.
> Je ne veux pas *de viande*.
> I don't want any (of it).
> Je n'*en* veux pas.

> We speak about the café.
> Nous parlons *du café*.
> We speak about it.
> Nous *en* parlons.

> They leave the restaurant.
> Elles sortent *du restaurant*.
> They leave (it) from there.
> Elles *en* sortent.

En is always expressed in French even though it may have no English equivalent or is not expressed in English:

> Do you have any money? Yes, I do.
> Avez-vous *de l'argent*? Oui, j'*en* ai.

En is placed before the verb to which its meaning is tied, usually before the conjugated verb. When there are two verbs, *en* is placed before the infinitive:

> He takes (eats) some. He wants to take (eat)
> Il *en* prend. some.
> Il désire *en* prendre.
>
> Don't take (eat) any.
> N'*en* prends pas.

In an affirmative command *en* changes position and is placed immediately after the verb and is joined to it by a hyphen:

> Take (eat) some! (Familiar)
> Prends-*en*! (*prahN zahN*)

Don't forget to ask for the check at the end of your meal:

> The check please.
> L'addition, s'il vous plaît.
> *lah-dee-syohN seel voo pleh*

You're a Social Butterfly

In This Chapter

- The verbs *vouloir* and *pouvoir*
- Amusements and diversions
- Invitations: extending, accepting, and refusing

You've had enough sightseeing and now you just want to relax and have some fun. You can go off to the ocean to swim and surf. Or do snow-covered mountains entice you to ski or hike? Are you a film buff or an opera lover? With the help of this chapter you'll be able to do it all and more, as well as be a guest or do the inviting.

I Love Sports!

Whether you like to relax as a beach bum, spend your days gazing out at the azure ocean, or feel compelled to engage in every fast-paced sport you can, you need certain words and terms to make your preferences known. Table 10.1 provides a list of sports and outdoor activities.

Table 10.1 Sports

One plays	On fait	*ObN feh*
aerobics	de l'aérobic *m.*	*duh lahy-roh-beek*
baseball	du base-ball	*dew bays-bohl*
basketball	du basket-ball	*dew bahs-keht bohl*
boating	du canotage	*dew kah-noh-tahzh*
cycling	du cyclisme	*dew see-kleez-muh*
fishing	de la pêche	*duh lah pehsh*
football	du football américain	*dew foot-bohl ah-may-ree-kaN*
golf	du golf	*dew gohlf*
horseback riding	de l'équitation *f.*	*duh lay-kee-tah-syohN*
hunting	de la chasse	*duh lah shahs*
jogging	du jogging	*dew zhoh-geeng*
sailing	du bateau à voiles	*dew bah-to ah vwahl*
scuba (skin) diving	de la plongée sous-marine	*duh lah plohN-zhay soo-mah-reen*
skating	du patin	*dew pah-taN*
skiing	du ski	*dew skee*
soccer	du football	*dew foot-bohl*
swimming	de la natation	*duh lah nah-tah-syohN*
tennis	du tennis	*dew tay-nees*
volleyball	du volley-ball	*dew voh-lee bohl*
waterskiing	du ski nautique	*dew skee no-teek*

Use the verb *faire* when talking about engaging in a sport.

> Vous faites du tennis? On fait de la pêche?
> Do you play tennis? How about going fishing?

The verbs *vouloir* (*voo-lwahr*/to want) and *pouvoir* (*poo-vwahr*/to be able to) are irregular and may be followed by the infinitive of a verb to invite someone along:

French	Pronunciation	English
je veux	*zhuh vuh*	I want
tu veux	*tew vuh*	you want
il veut	*eel vuh*	he wants
nous voulons	*noo voo-lohN*	we want
vous voulez	*voo voo-lay*	you want
ils veulent	*eel vuhl*	they want

French	Pronunciation	English
je peux	*zhuh puh*	I am able to (can)
tu peux	*tew puh*	you are able to (can)
il peut	*eel puh*	he is able to (can)
nous pouvons	*noo poo-vohN*	we are able to (can)
vous pouvez	*voo poo-vay*	you are able to (can)
ils peuvent	*eel puhv*	they are able to (can)

Vous voulez (Tu veux) + infinitive of a verb

Vous voulez (Tu veux) faire du patin?

Do you want to go skating?

Vous pouvez (Tu peux) + infinitive of a verb

Vous pouvez (Tu peux) aller à la pêche?

Can you go fishing?

An Extra Workout

Tell a friend in French which sports you like to participate in and which you prefer to watch on television. Then invite your friend along.

Other Amusement

If you're not into sports, there are plenty of other activities to keep you busy. The phrases in Table 10.2 will enable you to pursue other interests. Don't forget to bring along *les jumelles* (*lay zhew-mehl/* binoculars) should you choose attend the opera, ballet, theater, or a concert.

> I would like to go …
> Je voudrais aller …
> *zhuh voo-dreh zah-lay*

Table 10.2   Places to Go

English	French	Pronunciation
to the ballet	au ballet	*o bah-leh*
to the beach	à la plage	*ah lah plahzh*
to the casino	au casino	*o kah-zee-no*
to a concert	au concert	*o kohN-sehr*
to a discotheque	à une discothèque	*ah ewn dees-koh-tehk*
to the mall	au centre commercial	*o sahNtr koh-mehr-syahl*
to the movies	au cinéma	*o see-nay mah*
to the opera	à l'opéra	*ah loh-pay rah*
to the theater	au théâtre	*o tay-ahtr*
to take a hike	faire une randonnée	*fehr ewn rahN-doh-nay*

At the Movies and on TV

You're all played out, you're all worked out, and your tummy is full. If you're a film buff you may want to catch the latest film or even your favorite TV program. For some quiet entertainment, ask the following questions and consult Table 10.3.

What kind of film are they showing?
On passe quel genre de film?
ohN pahs kehl zhahNr duh feelm

What's on TV?
Qu'est-ce qu'il y a à la télé?
kehs keel yah ah lah tay-lay

Table 10.3   Movies and Television Programs

English	French	Pronunciation
adventure film	un film d'aventure	*uhN feelm dah-vahN-tewr*
cartoon	un dessin animé	*uhN deh-saN ah-nee-may*
comedy	un film comique	*uhN feelm koh-meek*
game show	un jeu	*uhN zhuh*
horror movie	un film d'horreur	*uhN feelm doh-ruhr*
love story	un film d'amour	*uhN feelm dah-moor*
mystery	un mystère	*uhN mees-tehr*
news	les informations *f.*	*lay zaN-fohr-mah-syohN*
police story	un film policier	*uhN feelm poh-lee-syay*
science-fiction film	un film de science-fiction	*uhN feelm duh see-ahNs-feek-syohN*
soap opera	un feuilleton (mélodramatique)	*uhN fuhy-tohN (may-loh-drah-mah-teek)*
spy movie	un film d'espionnage	*uhN feelm dehs-pee-yoh-nazh*
talk show	une causerie	*ewn koz-ree*
weather	la météo	*lay may-tay-o*

In French movie theaters, an usher, usually a young woman (une ouvreuse—*ewn oo-vruhz*) helps you select a seat to your liking and will expect a tip (un pourboire—*uhN poor-bwahr*) for services rendered. There are often at least 15 minutes of commercials shown before the main feature begins. At that time the usher comes around with a selection of candy and ice cream. Do you crave popcorn? Sorry, it's not sold! Refer to the following explanations when you choose a movie or theater:

INT-18 ans Interdit aux moins de 18 ans
Forbidden for those under 18

V.O. Version originale
Original version, subtitled

V.F. Version française
Dubbed in French

T.R. Tarif réduit
Reduced rate

C.V. Carte vermeille
"Red" senior citizens' card

Pl. Prix des places
Price of a seat

Expressing Your Opinion

If you like television, you might get hooked on *un feuilleton mélodramatique* (*uhN fuhy-tohN may-lo-drah-mah-teek*), a soap opera or any show that strikes your fancy. If you enjoy the program, you might say:

I love it!	J'adore!	*zhah-dohr*
It's a good movie.	C'est un bon film.	*seh tuhN bohN feelm*
It's amusing!	C'est amusant!	*seh tah-mew-zahN*
It's great!	C'est génial!	*seh zhay-nyahl*
It's moving!	C'est émouvant!	*seh tay-moo-vahN*
It's original!	C'est original!	*seh toh-ree-zhee-nahl*

If the show leaves something to be desired, try the following phrases:

I hate it!	Je déteste!	*zhuh day-tehst*
It's a bad movie!	C'est un mauvais film.	*seh tuhN mo-veh feelm*
It's a loser!	C'est un navet!	*seh tuhN nah-veh*
It's garbage!	C'est bidon!	*seh bee-dohN*
It's the same old thing!	C'est toujours la même chose!	*seh too-zhoor lah mehm shohz*
It's too violent!	C'est trop violent!	*seh tro vee-oh-lahN*

Invitations

It isn't much fun to play alone. Why not ask someone to join you? To extend an invitation, you can ask the following:

Would you like to join me (us)?
Voudriez-vous m'accompagner
(nous accompagner)?
*voo-dree-yay voo mah-kohN-pah-nyay
(noo zah-kohN-pah-nyay)*

Whether you've been invited to play a game, to spend time at the opera, or to just visit someone at home, the following phrases will allow you to graciously accept, to cordially refuse, or to show your indifference.

Accepting		
Avec plaisir.	*ah-vehk pleh-zeer*	With pleasure.
Bien entendu.	*byaN nahN-tahN-dew*	Of course.

Accepting

Bien sûr.	*byaN sewr*	Of course.
C'est une bonne idée.	*seh tewn bohn ee-day*	That's a good idea.
Chouette!	*shoo-eht*	Great!
D'accord.	*dah-kohr*	Okay. (I agree.)
Et comment!	*ay koh-mahN*	And how! You bet!
Il n'y a pas d'erreur.	*eel nyah pah deh-ruhr*	There's no doubt about it.
Pourquoi pas?	*poor-kwah pah*	Why not?
Si tu veux (vous voulez)	*see tew vuh (voo voo-lay)*	If you want to.
Volontiers!	*voh-lohN-tyay*	Gladly.

Refusing

C'est impossible.	*seh taN-poh-seebl*	It's impossible.
Encore!	*ahN-kohr*	Not again!
Je n'ai pas envie.	*zhuh nay pah zahN-vee*	I don't feel like it.
Je ne peux pas.	*zhuh nuh puh pah*	I can't.
Je ne suis pas libre.	*zhuh nuh swee pah leebr*	I'm not free.
Je ne veux pas.	*zhuh nuh vuh pah*	I don't want to.
Je regrette.	*zhuh ruh-greht*	I'm sorry.
Je suis désolé(e).	*zhuh swee day-zoh-lay*	I'm sorry.
Je suis fatigué(e).	*zhuh swee fah-tee-gay*	I'm tired.
Je suis occupé(e).	*zhuh swee zoh-kew-pay*	I'm busy.

Showing Indecision and Indifference

Ça dépend.	*sah day-pahN*	It depends.
Ça m'est égal.	*sah meh tay-gahl*	It's all the same to me.
Ce que tu préfères (vous préférez).	*suh kuh tew pray-fehr (voo pray-fay-ray)*	Whatever you want.
Comme tu veux (vous voulez).	*kohm tew vuh (voo voo-lay)*	Whatever you want.
Je n'ai pas de préférence.	*zhuh nay pas duh pray-fay-rahNs*	I don't have any preference.
Je ne sais pas trop.	*zhuh nuh seh pah tro*	I really don't know.
Peut-être.	*puh-tehtr*	Perhaps. Maybe.

Chapter 11

Personal Services

In This Chapter

- At the hairdresser's
- At the dry cleaner's and the Laundromat
- At the shoemaker's
- At the optician's
- At the jeweler's
- At the camera shop and other services

Good grief! Your roots are showing! You've spilled some ketchup on your new white shorts! Your left contact lens just ripped! Your toddler decided to play with your watch in the bathtub! What should you do? Don't worry. It's not a catastrophe. Just consult the concierge of your hotel or consult *les pages jaunes* (*lay pahzh zhon*/the yellow pages). Everything will work out in the end.

A Very Bad Hair Day!

Today's new unisex establishments have put an end to past tradition where men went *chez le coiffeur* (to the barber's) and women went *au salon de beauté* (to the beauty parlor). More and more, men and women are demanding similar services. To get what you want simply ask:

Could you give me ...   I would like ...
Pourriez-vous me donner ...   Je voudrais ...
poo-ryay voo muh doh-nay   *zhuh voo-dreh*

Today's salons provide the services listed in Table 11.1.

Table 11.1   At the Salon

English	French	Pronunciation
a facial	un massage facial	*uhN mah-sahzh fah-syahl*
a haircut	une coupe de cheveux	*ewn koop duh shuh-vuh*
a manicure	une manucure	*ewn mah-new-kewr*
a pedicure	une pédicurie	*ewn pay-dee-kew-ree*
a permanent	une permanente	*ewn pehr-mah-nahNt*
a rinse	un rinçage colorant	*uhN raN-sahzh koh-loh-rahN*
a set	une mise en plis	*ewn mee-zahN plee*
a shampoo	un shampooing	*uhN shahN-pwaN*
a trim	une coupe	*ewn koop*
a waxing	une épilation	*ewn ay-pee-lah-syohN*
highlights	des reflets	*day ruh-fleh*
layers	une coupe dégradée	*ewn koop day-grah-day*

Do you need other services? Table 11.2 provides the phrases you need to get them. Use the following phrase to preface your request:

Could you please ...?
Pourriez-vous ... s'il vous plaît?
poo-ryay voo ... seel voo pleh

Table 11.2   Other Services

English	French	Pronunciation
blow dry my hair	me donner un brushing	*muh doh-nay uhN bruh-sheeng*
curl my hair	me friser les cheveux	*muh free-zay lay shuh-vuh*
shave my beard (mustache)	me raser la barbe (la moustache)	*muh rah-zay lah bahrb (lah moo-stahsh)*
straighten my hair	me défriser les cheveux	*muh day-free-zay lay shuh-vuh*
trim my bangs	me rafraîchir la frange	*muh rah-freh-sheer lah frahNzh*
trim my beard (mustache, sideburns)	me rafraîchir la barbe (la moustache, les pattes)	*muh rah-freh-sheer lah bahrb (lah moo-stahsh, lay paht)*

Getting What You Want

When there's a language barrier, there's no end to the disasters that could befall you, as you try to get the cut, style, and color you desire. The following phrases will help you make yourself perfectly clear:

> I prefer my hair …
> Je préfère mes cheveux …
> *zhuh pray-fehr may shuh-vuh*

> I'd like a … style …
> Je voudrais une coiffure …
> *zhuh voo-dreh zewn kwah-fewr*

English	French	Pronunciation
long	longs	*lohN*
medium	mi-longs	*mee-lohN*
short	courts	*koor*
wavy	frisés	*free-zay*
curly	bouclés	*boo-klay*
straight	raides (lisses)	*rehd (lee-lees)*

Does your hair sometimes feel stiff and gooey after a stylist has coated it with mousse, gel, or spray? How do you feel about all those chemicals seeping into your skull? Are you allergic to certain products? If you don't want something on your hair, don't be afraid to tell the hairdresser.

> Don't put on any ... please.
> Ne mettez pas de (d') ... s'il vous plaît.
> *nuh meh-tay pah duh ... seel voo pleh*

English	French	Pronunciation
conditioner	après-shampooing	*ah-preh shahN-pwaN*
gel	gel coiffant *m.*	*zhehl kwah-fahN*
hairspray	laque *f.*	*lahk*
mousse	mousse coiffante *f.*	*moos kwah-fahN*
shampoo	shampooing *m.*	*shahN-pwaN*

Don't forget to ask about tipping:

> Is the tip included?
> Le service est compris?
> *luh sehr-vees eh kohN-pree*

Problems in General

Some handy, key phrases will help you in most situations. Keep them on hand whether you go to the dry cleaner, the shoemaker, the optometrist, the jeweler, or the camera store.

> At what time do you open (close)?
> Vous êtes ouvert (vous fermez) à quelle heure?
> *voo zeh too-vehr (voo fehr-may) ah kehl uhr*

What days are you open? Closed?
Vous êtes ouvert (vous fermez) quels jours?
voo zeh too-vehr (voo fehr-may) kehl zhoor

Can you fix ... for me?
Pouvez-vous me réparer ...?
poo-vay voo muh ray-pah-ray

Can you fix it (them) today?
Pouvez-vous le (la, l', les) réparer aujourd'hui?
poo-vay voo luh (lah, lay) ray-pah-ray o-zhoor-dwee

May I have a receipt?
Puis-je avoir un reçu?
pweezh ah-vwahr uhN ruh-sew

Can you fix it (them) temporarily (while I wait)?
Pouvez-vous le (la, l', les) réparer provisoire-
ment (pendant que j'attends)?
*poo-vay voo luh (lah, lay) ray-pah-ray proh-vee-
zwahr-mahN (pahN-dahN kuh zhah-tahN)*

How much do I owe you?
Je vous dois combien?
zhuh voo dwah kohN-byaN

At the Dry Cleaner's—à la Teinturerie

I don't like that rumpled look—like I slept in my
clothes for a week. I'm embarrassed by ugly stains
that I've overlooked—you know, those yellow ones
that always seem to crop up on white clothes. Don't
despair. If you know how to express yourself, your
stains, spots, tears, and wrinkles will be history.

I have a problem.   What's the problem?
J'ai un problème.   Quel est le problème?
zhay uhN proh-blehm   *kehl eh luh proh-blehm*

There is (are) …
Il y a …
eel yah

English	French	Pronunciation
a hole	un trou	*uhN troo*
a missing button	un bouton qui manque	*uhN boo-tohN kee mahNk*
a spot	une tache	*ewn tahsh*
a tear	une déchirure	*ewn day-shee-rewr*

Once the problem has been explained, state what you'd like done about it:

Can you (dry) clean this (these) … for me?
Vous pouvez me nettoyer (à sec) ce (cette, cet, ces) …?
voo poo-vay muh neh-twah-yay ah sehk suh (seht, seht, say)

Can you please mend this (these) … for me?
Vous pouvez me faire recoudre ce (cette, cet, ces) …?
voo poo-vay muh fehr ruh-koodr suh (seht, seht, say)

Can you please press (repair) this (these) … for me?
Vous pouvez me repasser (réparer) ce (cette, cet, ces) …?
voo poo-vay muh ruh-pah-say (ray-pah-ray) suh (seht, seht, say)

Can you please starch this (these) ... for me?
Vous pouvez m'amidonner ce (cette, cet, ces) ...?
voo poo-vay mah-mee-doh-nay suh (seht, seht, say)

I need it (them) ...
J'en ai besoin ...
zhahN nay buh-zwaN

today	this afternoon
aujourd'hui	cet après-midi
o-zhoor-dwee	*seh tah-preh mee-dee*
tonight	tomorrow
ce soir	demain
suh swahr	*duh-maN*
the day after tomorrow	next week
après-demain	la semaine prochaine
ah-preh duh-maN	*lah suh-mehn proh-shehn*

At the Laundromat—à la Blanchisserie/ à la Laverie Automatique

Laundry piles up quickly when you're on vacation. If it can't wait till you get home, a trip to a Laundromat could save you a bundle. Use the following phrases to get the information you need.

I'd like to wash my clothes.
Je voudrais laver mes vêtements.
zhuh voo-dreh lah-vay may veht-mahN

I'd like to have my clothes washed.
Je voudrais faire laver mes vêtements.
zhuh voo-dreh fehr lah-vay may veht-mahN

Are you mortified by that ring around your collar?
Or perhaps you're afraid that your beautiful new silk
shirt will get ruined by an amateur. If you're intent
on doing the job yourself, use the following phrases:

Is there a free washing machine (dryer)?
Y a-t-il une machine à laver (un séchoir) libre?
ee ah-tee ewn mah-sheen ah lah-vay (uhN saysh-wahr) leebr

Where can I buy soap powder?
Où puis-je acheter de la lessive en poudre?
oo pweezh ahsh-tay duh lah leh-seev ahN poodr

At the Shoemaker's–Chez le Cordonnier

Your shoelace broke, you've worn a hole in the sole
of your shoe from walking so much, or you just need
a good shine. Use the following phrases to help you.

Can you repair ... for me?
Pouvez-vous me réparer ...?
poo-vay voo muh ray-pah-ray

these shoes	these boots
ces chaussures	ces bottes
say sho-sewr	*say boht*
this heel	this sole
ce talon	cette semelle
suh tah-lohN	*seht suh-mehl*

Do you sell shoelaces?
Vendez-vous des lacets?
vahN-day-voo day lah-seh

I'd like a shoe shine.
Je voudrais un cirage.
zhuh voo-dreh zuhN see-rage

When can I have them?
Quand puis-je les avoir?
kahN pweezh lay zah-vwahr

I need them by Friday (without fail).
Il me les faut vendredi (sans faute, assurément).
eel muh lay fo vahN-druh-dee (sahN fot, ah-sew-ray-mahN)

At the Optometrist's—Chez l'Opticien

For those who are visually challenged, losing or tearing a pair of contacts, or breaking a frame or lens of a pair of glasses could prove a disaster. If you depend on optical necessities, familiarize yourself with the following phrases:

Can you repair these glasses for me?
Pouvez-vous me réparer ces lunettes?
poo-vay voo muh ray-pah-ray say lew-neht

The lens (the frame) is broken.
Le verre (la monture) est cassé(e).
luh vehr (lah mohN-tewr) eh kah-say

Can you tighten the screws?
Pouvez-vous resserrer les vis?
poo-vay voo ruh-seh-ray lay vees

Can you replace this contact lens?
Pouvez-vous remplacer cette lentille (ce verre)
de contact?
*poo-vay voo rahN-plah-say seht lahN-tee-y
(suh vehr) duh kohN-tahkt*

I need the glasses (contacts) as soon as possible.
Il me faut les lunettes (les verres de contact)
aussitôt que possible.
*eel muh fo lay lew-neht (lay vehr duh kohN-tahkt)
o-see-to kuh poh-seebl*

Do you sell sunglasses?
Vendez-vous des lunettes de soleil?
vahN-day voo day lew-neht duh soh-lehy

At the Jeweler's—Chez le Bijoutier

What luck! Your watch has gone haywire in the
middle of your trip. Use the following phrases if
you need it repaired before returning home:

Can you repair this watch?
Pouvez-vous réparer cette montre?
poo-vay voo ray-pah-ray seht mohNtr

My watch doesn't work.
Ma montre ne marche pas.
mah mohNtr nuh mahrsh pah

My watch is fast (slow).
Ma montre avance (retarde).
Mah mohNtr ah-vahNs (ruh-tahrd)

Do you sell bands (batteries)?
Vendez-vous des bandes (des piles)?
vahN-day voo day bahnd (day peel)

When will it be ready?
Quand sera-t-elle prête?
kahN suh-rah tehl preht

At the Camera Shop—au Magasin de Photographie

When we're on a fabulous vacation, it's very important to most of us to capture on film those special moments and unforgettable landscapes. If you need to visit a camera shop or film store in a French speaking country, the following words and phrases will come in handy.

a camera
un appareil-photo
uhN nah-pah-rehy foh-to

a video
un appareil vidéo camera
uhN nah-pah-rehy vee-day-o

If you have special needs, you might ask:

Can you fix this camera?
Pouvez-vous réparer cet appareil-photo?
poo-vay voo ray-pah-ray seht ah-pah-rehy-foh-to

The film doesn't advance.
Le film n'avance pas.
luh feelm nah-vahns pah

I need a new battery.
Il me faut une nouvelle pile.
eel muh fo tewn noo-vehl peel

How much will the repair cost?
Combien coûtera la réparation?
kohN-byaN koot-rah lah ray-pah-rah-syohN

I need it as soon as possible.
J'en ai besoin aussitôt que possible.
zhaN nay buh-zwaN o-see-to kuh poh-seebl

Do you sell rolls of 20 (36) exposure film in color (black and white)?
Vendez-vous des pellicules de vingt (trente-six) en couleur (noir et blanc)?
vahN-day voo day peh-lee-kewl duh vaN (trahNt-sees) ahN koo-luhr (nwahr ay blahN)

There's a Doctor on Call

In This Chapter

- All about your body
- Signs, symptoms, and illnesses
- Saying how long you've felt this way
- Reflexive verbs
- At the pharmacy

Invariably at the worst possible moment, people get sick or have accidents. The situation can become difficult, if not critical when you can't communicate the problem. In this chapter, you will learn how to explain your ailments and how long you've been experiencing the symptoms.

Does It Hurt Here or There?

When traveling, it pays to be prepared in case illness strikes. Start by familiarizing yourself with the parts of the body in Table 12.1.

Table 12.1 Parts of the Body

English	French	English	French
arm	le bras (*luh brah*)	kidney	le rein (*luh raN*)
back	le dos (*luh do*)	knee	le genou (*luh zhuh-noo*)
chest	la poitrine	leg	la jambe (*lah zhahNb*)
ear	l'oreille *f.* (*loh-rehy*) (*lah pwah-treen*)	lip	la lèvre (*lah lehvr*)
		lung	le poumon (*luh poo-mohN*)
elbow	le coude (*luh kood*)	mouth	la bouche (*lah boosh*)
eye	l'oeil *m.* (*luhy*)	neck	le cou (*luh koo*)
eyes	les yeux (*lay zyuh*)	nose	le nez (*luh nay*)
face	la figure, le visage (*lah fee-gewr, luh vee-zahzh*)	shoulder	l'épaule (*lay-pohl*)
finger	le doigt (*luh dwah*)	stomach	l'estomac *m.* (*leh-stoh-mah*)
foot	le pied (*luh pyay*)	throat	la gorge (*lah gohrzh*)
hand	la main (*lah maN*)	toe	l'orteil *m.* (*lohr-tehy*)
head	la tête (*lah teht*)	tongue	la langue (*lah lahNg*)
heart	le coeur (*luh kuhr*)	tooth	la dent (*lah dahN*)
hip	la hanche (*lah ahNsh*)	wrist	le poignet (*luh pwah-nyeh*)

If you run into a problem and have to seek medical attention, the obvious first question will be: "What's the matter with you?", "Qu'est-ce que vous avez?" (*kehs kuh voo zah-vay*). To say what hurts or bothers you, use the expression *avoir mal à* + definite article:

> Do you have a stomach ache?
> Tu as mal à l'estomac?
> *tew ah ah lehs-toh-mah*

> Our feet hurt.
> Nous avons mal aux pieds.
> *noo zah-vohN mahl o pyay*

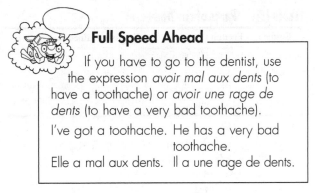

Full Speed Ahead

If you have to go to the dentist, use the expression *avoir mal aux dents* (to have a toothache) or *avoir une rage de dents* (to have a very bad toothache).

I've got a toothache. He has a very bad toothache.

Elle a mal aux dents. Il a une rage de dents.

What Are Your Symptoms?

If you need to provide a more detailed description of your aches and pains, use the symptoms and conditions listed in Table 12.2. Use the phrase *J'ai* (*zhay*/I have) to preface your complaint.

Table 12.2   Symptoms

English	French	Pronunciation
bruise	une contusion	*ewn kohN-tew-zyohN*
bump	une bosse	*ewn bohs*
burn	une brûlure	*ewn brew-lewr*
chills	des frissons	*day free-sohN*
cough	une toux	*ewn too*
cramps	des crampes	*day krahNp*
cut	une coupure	*ewn koo-pewr*
diarrhea	de la diarrhée	*dun lah dee-ah-ray*
fever	de la fièvre	*duh lah fyehvr*
fracture	une fracture	*ewn frahk-tewr*
lump	une grosseur	*ewn groh-suhr*
pain	une douleur	*ewn doo-luhr*

continues

Table 12.2 Symptoms continued

English	French	Pronunciation
rash	une éruption	*ewn nay-rewp-syohN*
sprain	une foulure	*ewn foo-lewr*
swelling	une enflure	*ewn nahN-flewr*
wound	une blessure	*ewn bleh-sewr*

Here are some other phrases that might prove useful when explaining how you're feeling:

I'm coughing.
Je tousse.
zhuh toos

I'm sneezing.
J'éternue.
zay-tehr-new

I'm bleeding.
Je saigne.
zhuh seh-nyuh

I'm constipated.
Je suis constipé(e).
zhuh swee kohN-stee-pay

I'm nauseous.
J'ai des nausées.
zhay day no-zay

I have trouble sleeping.
J'ai du mal à dormir.
zhay dew mahl ah dohr-meer

I feel bad.
Je me sens mal.
zhuh muh sahN mahl

I hurt everywhere.
J'ai mal partout.
zhay mahl pahr-too

I feel weak.
Je me sens faible.
zhuh muh sahN fehbl

I'm dizzy.
J'ai le vertige.
zhay luh vehr-teezh

The Doctor Wants to Know

You might have to answer many personal questions about your general health and family history so the doctor can treat you properly. Refer to Table 12.3 for the words you'll need.

Have you had ...?
Avez-vous subi (eu) ...?
ah-vay voo sew-bee(ew)

Do you suffer from ...?
Souffrez-vous de (d') ...?
soo-fray voo duh

Table 12.3   Other Symptoms and Illness

English	French	Pronunciation
allergic reaction	une réaction allergique	*ewn ray-ahk-syohN ah-lehr-zheek*
angina	une angine	*ewn nahN-zheen*
appendicitis	l'appendicite *f.*	*lah-pahN-dee-seet*
asthma	l'asthme *m.*	*lahz-muh*
bronchitis	la bronchite	*lah brohN-sheet*
cancer	le cancer	*luh kahN-sehr*
diabetes	le diabète	*luh dee-ah-beht*
dizziness	le vertige	*luh vehr-teezh*
hay fever	le rhume des foins	*luh rewm day fwaN*
heart attack	une crise cardiaque	*ewn kreez kahr-dyahk*
hepatitis	l'hépatite	*lay-pah-teet*
pneumonia	la pneumonie	*lah pnuh-moh-nee*
stroke	une attaque d'apoplexie	*ewn nah-tahk dah-poh-plehk-see*
tuberculosis	la tuberculose	*lah tew-behr-kew-lohz*

Remember to give the doctor any pertinent information that might help him/her serve you better. You might need some of the following phrases:

I've had this pain since ...
J'ai cette douleur depuis ...
zhay seht doo-luhr duh-pwee

There's a (no) family history of …
Il (n') y a (pas) de fréquence de …
eel (nyah) yah (pah) duh fray-kahNs duh

I am (not) allergic to …
Je (ne) suis (pas) allérgique à …
zhuh (nuh) swee (pah) (zah-lehr-geek) ah

I had …	… years ago.
J'ai subi …	il y a … ans.
zhay sew-bee …	*eel yah …ahN*

I'm taking …	I'm pregnant.
Je prends …	Je suis enceinte.
zhuh prahN	*zhuh swee zahN-saNt*

Want to know how serious it is? Ask the following:

Is it serious?	Is it contagious?
C'est grave?	C'est contagieux?
seh grahv	*seh kohN-tah-zhyuh*

How often do I take this medicine?
Combien de fois par jour faut-il prendre ce médicament?
kohN-byaN duh fwah pahr zhoor fo-teel prahNdr suh may-dee-kah-mahN

How long do I have to stay in bed?
Combien de temps dois-je garder le lit?
kohN-byaN duh tahN dwahzh gahr-day luh lee

May I please have a receipt for my medical insurance?
Puis-je avoir une quittance pour mon assurance maladie?
pweezh ah-vwahr ewn kee-tahNs poor mohN nah-sew rahNs mah-lah-dee

How Long Has This Been Going On?

Doctors always ask how long you've been experiencing your symptoms. This information is extremely important for a correct diagnosis. The phrases in Table 12.4 suggest the number of ways you may hear the question posed and the ways in which to answer the question.

Table 12.4   How Long Have Your Symptoms Lasted?

Question	Answer
Since when … Depuis quand … *duh-pwee kahN*	Since … Depuis … *duh-pwee*
How long has (have) … been … Depuis combien de temps … *duh-pwee kohN-byaN duh tahN*	For … Depuis … *duh-pwee*
How long has (have) … been … Combien de temps y a-t-il que … *kohN-byaN duh tahN ee ah-teel kuh*	For … Il y a + time + que … *eel yah + time + kuh*
How long has (have) … been … Ça fait combien de temps que … *sah feh kohN-byaN duh tahN kuh* Voilà + time + que	For … Ça fait + time + que … *sah feh + time + kuh,* *vwah-lah + time + que*
How long have you been suffering? Depuis combien de temps souffrez-vous? *duh-pwee kohN-byaN duh tahN soo-fray voo*	For three days. Depuis trois jours. *duh-pwee trwah zhoor*
Since when have you been suffering? Depuis quand souffrez-vous? *duh-pwee kahN soo-fray voo*	Since yesterday. Depuis hier. *duh-pwee yehr*
How long have you been suffering? Combien de temps y a-t-il que vous souffrez? *kohN-byaN duh tahN ee ah-teel kuh* *voo soo-fray*	For two days. Il y a deux jours. *eel yah duh zhoor*

continues

Table 12.4   How Long Have Your Symptoms Lasted?
continued

Question	Answer
How long have you been suffering? Ça fait combien de temps que vous souffrez? *sah feh kohN-byaN duh tahN kuh voo soo-fray*	It's been a week./ For a week. Ça fait une semaine/ Voilà une semaine. *sah feh tewn suh-mehn/ vwah-lah ewn suh-mehn*

An Extra Workout

Practice having an imaginary conversation with a doctor. Describe how you feel, your symptoms, and how long you've felt this way.

Reflexive Verbs

A reflexive verb shows that the subject is performing an action upon itself and can always be identified by the pronoun *se* that precedes the infinitive. The subject and the reflexive pronoun refer to the same person(s) or thing(s): *She* hurt *herself. They* enjoy *themselves.*

Use the following pronouns when the verb is reflexive. Put these pronouns in the same position as direct and indirect object pronouns, *y* and *en:*

me (myself)	nous (ourselves)
te (yourself)	vous (yourself[selves])
se (him/herself)	se (themselves)

At the Pharmacy

In general, when traveling outside the United States, you should not expect to find a pharmacy that carries the wide range of supplies found in many of our drug stores: stationery, cards, cosmetics, candy, and household items. In France, *a pharmacie* is easily identified by a green cross above the door. It sells prescription drugs, over-the-counter medications, items intended for personal hygiene, and some cosmetics. If the pharmacy is closed, look for a sign on the door telling customers where they can locate a neighboring pharmacy that is open all night *(une pharmacie de garde).*

A *droguerie* sells chemical products, paints, household cleansers and accessories (mops, brooms, buckets), and some hygiene and beauty products, but does not dispense prescriptions.

A *drugstore* is like a small department store; it stocks personal hygiene items, books, magazines, newspapers, records, maps, guides, gifts and souvenirs, but no prescription medicine. Additionally, you may also find fast food restaurants, a bar, and even a movie theater.

If you are indeed trying to find the closest drugstore, you might want to ask:

> Where's the nearest pharmacy?
> Où est la pharmacie la plus proche?
> *oo eh lah fahr-mah-see lah plew prohsh*

When you speak to the druggist, you would say:

Could you please fill this prescription (immediately)?
Pourriez-vous exécuter (tout de suite) cette ordonnance, s'il vous plaît?
poo-ryay voo ehg-zay-kew-tay (toot sweet) seh tohr-doh-nahNs seel voo pleh

How long will it take?
Ça prendra combien de temps?
sah prahN-drah kohN-byaN duh tahN

For your over the counter needs, consult Table 12.5 which will help you find them. Begin by saying to a clerk:

Je cherche … (*zhuh shersh*/I'm looking for …)

Table 12.5 Drugstore Items

English	French	Pronunciation
alcohol	de l'alcool	*duh lahl-kohl*
antacid	un anti-acide	*uhN nahN-tee ah-seed*
antihistamine	un antihistaminique	*uhN nahn-tee-ees-tah-mee-neek*
antiseptic	un antiseptique	*uhN nahN-tee-sehp-teek*
aspirins	des aspirines	*day zah-spee-reen*
bandages (wound)	des pansements *m.*	*day pahNs-mahN*
Band-aid	un pansement adhésif	*uhn pahNs-mahN ahd-ay-zeef*
bobby pins	des épingles à cheveux *f.*	*day zay-paNgl ah shuh-vuh*
bottle	un biberon	*uhN beeb-rohN*
brush	une brosse	*ewn brohs*
cleansing cream	une crème démaquillante	*ewn krehm day-mah-kee-yahNt*

English	French	Pronunciation
comb	un peigne	*uhN peh-nyuh*
condoms	des préservatifs *m.*	*day pray-zehr-vah-teef*
cotton (absorbent)	du coton de l'ouate	*dew koh-tohN duh lwaht*
cough drops	des pastilles *f.*	*day pah-stee-y*
cough syrup	le sirop contre la toux	*luh see-roh kohNtr lah too*
deodorant	du déodorant	*dew day-oh-doh-rahN*
diapers (disposable)	des couches (disponibles) *m.*	*day koosh dees-poh-neebl*
emery boards	des limes à ongles	*day leem ah ohNgl*
eye drops	les gouttes pour les yeux, du collyre	*lay goot poor lay zyuh, dew koh-leer*
gauze pads	des bandes de gaze *f.*	*day bahnd duh gahz*
heating pad	un thermoplasme	*uhN tehr-moh-plahz-muh*
ice pack	une vessie de glace	*ewn veh-see duh glahs*
laxative (mild)	un laxatif (léger)	*uhN lahk-sah-teef (lay-zhay)*
makeup	du maquillage	*dew mah-kee-yahzh*
mouthwash	un dentifrice	*uhN dahN-tee-frees*
nail clippers	un coupe-ongles	*uhN koop ohNgl*
nail file	une lime à ongles	*ewn leem ah ohNgl*
nail polish remover	du dissolvant	*dew dee-sohl-vahN*
nose drops	des gouttes nasales *f.*	*day goot nah-zahl*
pacifier	une sucette	*ewn sew-seht*
razor (electric)	un rasoir (électrique)	*uhN rah-zwahr (ay-lehk-treek)*
razor blades	des lames de rasoir *f.*	*day lahm duh rah-zwahr*
safety pins	des épingles de sûreté *f.*	*day zay-paNgl duh sewr-tay*
sanitary napkins	des serviettes hygiéniques *f.*	*day sehr-vyeht ee-zhyay-neek*
shampoo anti-dandruff	du shampooing anti-pellicules	*dew shahN-pwaN ahN-tee peh-lee-kewl*
shaving cream	de la crème à raser	*duh lah krehm ah rah-zay*

continues

Table 12.5 Drugstore Items continued

English	French	Pronunciation
sleeping pills	des somnifères *m.*	*day sohm-nee-fehr*
soap (bar)	une savonette	*ewn sah-voh-neht*
suntan lotion	de la lotion solaire	*duh lah loh-syohN soh-lehr*
talcum powder	du talc	*dew tahlk*
tampons	des tampons périodiques *m.*	*day tahN-pohN pay-ree-oh-deek*
thermometer	un thermomètre	*uhN tehr-mo-mehtr*
tissues	des mouchoirs en papier *m.*	*day moosh-wahr ahN pah-pyay*
toothbrush	une brosse à dents	*ewn brohs ah dahN*
toothpaste	de la pâte dentifrice	*duh lah paht dahN-tee-frees*
tweezers	une pince à épiler	*ewn paNs ah ay-pee-lay*
vitamins	des vitamines *f.*	*day vee-tah-meen*

Special Items

For information or the rental of items for the physically challenged, listed in Table 12.6, go to a pharmacy that specializes in *la location d'appareils médiaux* (*lah loh-kah-syohn dah-pah-rehy may-dee-yo*).

Where can I get …?
Où puis-je obtenir …?
oo pweezh ohb-tuh-neer

Table 12.6   Special Needs

English	French	Pronunciation
cane	une canne	*ewn kahn*
crutches	des béquilles	*day bay-kee*
walker	un déambulateur	*uhN day-ahN-bew-lah-tuhr*
wheelchair	un fauteuil roulant	*uhN fo-tuhy roo-lahN*

Full Speed Ahead

Put French labels on the drugstore items you keep in stock. Every time you open the door to your medicine cabinet, memorize the name of at least two items you frequently use.

Chapter 13

Taking Care of Business

In This Chapter

- How to make a phone call
- Dealing with your mail
- Faxes, photocopies, and computers

Conducting business in a foreign country is always a bit of a challenge. It's crucial to understand how to place a phone call, send a letter, buy necessary stationery supplies, and deal with faxes and photocopies. Being computer literate in any language is probably one of the most important skills you'll need to possess. This chapter will help you deal with it all.

Phone Calls

If you plan to call long distance from a foreign country, whether for business or for pleasure, expect that someone will have to explain how to use the local phone system. It is also quite probable that the procedures for making local calls will be different from what you are accustomed to back home.

You will want to make sure to correctly express the type of call you want to make. Public pay phones are located in some post offices, cafés, and stores, and are on the streets of larger cities. Table 13.1 provides you with some options.

Table 13.1 Types of Phone Calls

English	French	Pronunciation
collect call	la communication en P.C.V.	*lah koh-mew-nee-kah-syohN ahN pay-say-vay*
credit-card call	la communication par carte de crédit	*lah koh-mew-nee-kah-syohN pahr kahrt duh kray-dee*
local call	la communication locale	*lah koh-mew-nee-kah-syohN loh-kahl*
long-distance call	la communication interurbaine	*lah koh-mew-nee-kah-syohN aN-tehr-ewr-behn*
out of the country call	la communication à l'étranger	*lah koh-mew-nee-kah-syohN ah lay-trahN-zhay*
person-to-person call	la communication avec préavis	*lah koh-mew-nee-kah-syohN ah-vehk pray-ah-vee*

Table 13.2 provides the words to help you understand French directions for placing a phone call.

Table 13.2 How to Make a Phone Call

English	French	Pronunciation
to call	téléphoner, appeler	*tay-lay-foh-nay, ah-play*
to call back	rappeler, retéléphoner	*rah-play, ruh-tay-lay-fohn-nay*
to dial	composer (faire) le numéro	*kohN-po-zay (fehr) luh new-may-ro*
to hang up (the receiver)	raccrocher, quitter	*rah-kroh-shay, kee-tay*
to insert the card	introduire la carte	*aN-troh-dweer lah kahrt*

English	French	Pronunciation
to know the area code	savoir l'indicatif, du pays (country), de la ville (city)	*sah-vwahr laN-dee-kah-teef, dew pay-ee, duh lah veel*
to leave a message	laisser un message	*leh-say uhN meh-sahzh*
to listen for the dial tone	attendre la tonalité	*ah-tahNdr lah toh-nah-lee-tay*
to pick up (the receiver)	décrocher	*day-kroh-shay*
to telephone	téléphoner, appeler par téléphone, donner un coup de fil	*tay-lay-foh-nay, ah-play pahr tay-lay-fohn, doh-nay uhN koo duh feel*

Phone Talk

Understanding telephone replies in a foreign language is far more difficult than face-to-face conversations, because you're not able to observe a person's body language. Additionally, telephones tend to distort voices and sounds. It would be wise for you to familiarize yourself with the expressions used when making and answering a phone call. Table 13.3 will show you how to begin a telephone conversation.

Table 13.3 Making a Phone Call

Calling	Answering
hello	hello
allô	allô
(*ah-lo*)	(*ah-lo*)
Is this the … residence?	Who's calling?
Je suis bien chez …?	Qui est à l'appareil?
(*zhuh swee byaN shay*)	(*kee eh tah lah-pah-rehy*)

continues

Table 13.3   Making a Phone Call   continued

Calling	Answering
It's ...	This is ...
C'est ...	Ici ...
(seh)	*(ee-see)*
Is ... in *(there)*?	Hold on.
... est là?	Ne quittez (quitte) pas.
(eh lah)	*(nuh kee-tay (keet) pah)*
	Just a moment.
	Un moment.
	(uhN moh-mahN)
I would like to speak to ...	He (She) is not in.
Je voudrais parler à ...	Il (Elle) n'est pas là.
(zhuh voo-dreh pahr-lay ah)	*(eel [ehl] neh pah lah)*
When will he (she) be back?	Do you want to leave a message?
Quand sera-t-il (elle) de	Voulez-vous (veux-tu) laisser un
retour?	message?
*(kahN suh-rah-teel [tehl] duh	*(voo-lay voo [vuh-tew] leh-say*
ruh-toor)*	*uhN meh-sahzh)*
I'll call back later.	
Je vais rappeler plus tard.	
(zhuh veh rah-play plew tahr)	

Attention!

Use *allô* to say hello when you answer the phone. *Bonjour* is used when greeting someone in person.

Problems

Are you having trouble reaching your party? The following are some phrases you might say or hear when you are having problems:

What number are you calling?
Vous demandez quel numéro?
voo duh-mahN-day kehl new-may-ro

It's a mistake.
C'est une erreur.
seh tewn eh-ruhr

(I have) You have the wrong number.
(J'ai) Vous avez le mauvais numéro.
(zhay) voo zah-vay luhmoh-veh new-may-ro

What's the problem?
Quel en est le problème?
kehl ahN neh luh proh-blehm

We got cut off (disconnected).
On nous a coupés.
ohN noo zah koo-pay

Please redial the number.
Recomposez le numéro, s'il vous plaît.
ruh-kohN-poh-zay luh new-may-ro seel voo pleh

The telephone is out of order.
Le téléphone est en panne (hors de service).
luh tay-lay-fohn eh tahN pahn (tohr duh sehr-vees)

There's a lot of static on the line.
Il y a beaucoup de parasites sur la ligne.
eel yah bo-koo duh pah-rah-seet sewr lah lee-nyuh

I'll Write, Instead

It's far more cost effective to send a letter than to place a long-distance call. Table 13.4 provides the vocabulary you need to send your mail.

Table 13.4 Mail and Post Office Terms

English	French	Pronunciation
address	l'adresse	*lah-drehs*
addressee	le destinataire	*luh dehs-tee-nah-tehr*
air letter	l'aérogramme *m.*	*lahy-roh-grahm*
envelope	l'enveloppe *f.*	*lahN-vlohp*
letter	la lettre	*lah lehtr*
mailbox	la boîte aux lettres	*lah bwaht o lehtr*
money order	le mandat-poste	*luh mahN-dah pohst*
package	le paquet	*luh pah-keh*
postcard	la carte postale	*lah kahrt pohs-tahl*
postage	l'affranchissement *m.*	*lah-frahN-shees-mahN*
postal code	le code postal (régional)	*luh kohd pohs-tahl (ray-zhoh-nahl)*
rate	le tarif	*luh tah-reef*
sheet of stamps	la feuille de timbres	*lah fuhy duh taNbr*
stamp	le timbre	*luh taNbr*

In France, many post offices open as early as 8 A.M., close as late as 7 P.M., and may take a two hour lunch break! There is a main branch in Paris which is always open. Stamps may be purchased at some *cafés*, *bureaux de tabac*, and *hôtels*. If you don't want to take a trip to the post office, look for a yellow mailbox.

Getting Service

You've written all the letters and postcards you felt obligated to write and now you're ready to send them off. If you don't know where a post office or mailbox is located, simply ask:

Where is the nearest post office (mailbox)?
Où se trouve (est) le bureau de poste le plus
proche (la boîte aux lettres la plus proche)?
*oo suh troov (eh) luh bew-ro duh pohst luh plew
prohsh (lah bwaht o lehtr lah plew prohsh)*

Depending upon the type of letters and packages
you wish to send, special forms, paperwork, and
postage rates are necessary. It is important to know
how to ask for the type of service you need:

What is the postage rate for ...?
Quel est le tarif de l'affranchissement pour ...?
kehl eh luh tah-reef duh lah-frahN-shees-mahN poor

a foreign country	the United States
(for overseas)	les Etats-Unis
l'étranger	*lay zay-tah zew-nee*
lay-trahN-zhay	

an air mail letter
une lettre envoyée par avion
ewn lehtr ahN-vwah-yay pahr ah-vyohN

a registered letter
une lettre recommandée
ewn lehtr ruh-koh-mahN-day

a special delivery letter
une lettre par exprès
ewn lehtr pahr ehks-preh

I would like to send this letter (this package) ...
Je voudrais envoyer cette lettre (ce paquet) ...
*zhuh voo-dreh zahN-vwah-yay seht lehtr
(suh pah-keh)*

by regular mail   by air mail
par courrier régulier par avion
pahr koo-ryay ray- *pahr ah-vyohN*
gew-lyay

by special delivery
par exprès
pahr ehks-preh

C.O.D.
livrable contre remboursement
(payable à l'arrivée)
lee-vrahbl kohNtr rahN-boors-mahN
(peh-yahbl ah lah-ree-vay)

How much does this letter (package) weigh?
Combien pèse cette lettre (ce paquet)?
kohN-byaN pehz seht lehtr (suh pah-keh)

When will it arrive?
Quand arrivera-t-elle (il)?
kahN tah-ree-vrah tehl (teel)

Faxes, Photocopies, and Computers

If you want your business to run smoothly, you just
cannot do without these three essential items: faxes,
photocopy machines, and computers. Use the phrases
in the following sections to help you operate these
machines in your business ventures.

Making Photocopies

I recently left the country to get some material for
this book. I pestered a lot of people, but I got just

about everything I needed. As luck would have it, when I went to the hotel's business center to have photocopies made, all the machines were down. Off I trudged to the nearest photocopy store. If this happens to you, here's what you might want to say:

I would like to make a photocopy of this paper (this document).

Je voudrais faire une photocopie de ce papier (ce document).

zhuh voo-dreh fehr ewn foh-to-koh-pee duh suh pah-pyay (suh doh-kew-mahN)

What is the cost per page?

Quel est le prix par page?

kehl eh luh pree pahr pahzh

Can you enlarge it (by 50 percent)?

Pouvez-vous l'élargir (de cinquante pour cent)?

poo-vay voo lay-lahr-zheer (duh saN-kahNt poor sahN)

Can you reduce it (by 25 percent)?

Pouvez-vous le réduire (de vingt-cinq pour cent)?

poo-vay vous luh ray-dweer (duh vaN-saNk poor sahN)

Can you make a color copy?

Pouvez-vous en faire une copie en couleurs?

poo-vay voo zahN fehr ewn koh-pee ahN koo-luhr

Fax It

Let's face it, a fax machine is becoming almost as important as a telephone in many households.

Frankly, it still boggles my mind that they are so easy to use. They can be a real convenience, when you least expect it. When you can transmit and receive messages and information in a matter of seconds or minutes, you can speed up the time it takes to transact business. That translates into extra cash. If you are conducting business in a French-speaking country, it's a must to be fax-literate.

> Do you have a fax machine?
> Avez-vous un télécopieur?
> *ah-vay voo uhN tay-lay-kohp-yuhr*

> I'd like to send a fax.
> Je voudrais transmettre une télécopie.
> *zhuh voo-dreh trahNz-mehtr ewn tay-lay-koh-pee*

> May I fax this letter (document) (to you)?
> Puis-je (vous) transmettre une télécopie de cette lettre (de ce document)?
> *pweezh (voo) trahNz-mehtr ewn koh-pee duh seht lehtr (duh suh doh-kew-mahN)*

> Fax it to me.
> Envoyez-m'en (Envoie-m'en) une télécopie.
> *ahN-vwah-yay mahN (ahN-vwah mahN) ewn tay-lay-koh-pee*

> I didn't get your fax.
> Je n'ai pas reçu votre télécopie.
> *zhuh nay pah ruh-sew vohtr tay-lay-koh-pee*

> Did you receive my fax?
> Avez-vous reçu ma télécopie?
> *ah-vay voo ruh-sew mah tay-lay-koh-pee*

Your fax is illegible.
Votre télécopie n'est pas lisible.
vohtr tay-lay-koh-pee neh pah lee-zeebl

Please send it again.
Veuillez la transmettre de nouveau.
vuh-yay lah trahNz-mehtr duh noo-vo

Please confirm that you've received my fax.
Veuillez confirmer la réception de ma télécopie.
*vuh-yay kohN-feer-may lah ray-sehp-syohN duh
mah tay-lay-koh-pee*

I'm a Computer Geek

In today's fast-paced world you must have some
computer knowledge in order to conduct your business. It's important to know what system, programs,
and peripherals other businesses are using. Will your
word processors and spread sheets be compatible?
Can you network? The phrases that follow will help
you, even if you're not a computer geek.

What kind of computer do you have?
Quel système (type, genre) d'ordinateur avez-
vous?
*kehl sees-tehm (teep, zhahNr) dohr-dee-nah-tuhr
ah-vay voo*

What operating system are you using?
Quel système opérant employez-vous?
kehl sees-tehm oh-pay-rahN ahN-plwah-yay-voo

What word processing program are you using?
Quel système de traitement de texte employez-vous?

kehl sees-tehm duh treht-mahN duh tehkst ahN-plwah-yay-voo

What spread sheet program are you using?
Quel tableur employez-vous?

kehl tah-bluhr ahN-plwah-yay-voo

What peripherals do you have?
Quels périphériques avez-vous?

kehl pay-ree-fay-reek ah-vay voo

Chapter 14

In Case of an Emergency

In This Chapter

- Expressing a problem
- Getting and offering help
- Getting to the right place

As vacation time approaches, television ads bombard us with warnings about being vigilant and careful travelers. Unfortunately, no matter how hard we try, sometimes we are distracted and careless with our personal belongings or we fall prey to crime or illness. These annoying and sometimes disastrous occurrences often happen at the most inopportune moments. When traveling abroad it is wise to have a general working knowledge of words and expressions that can help you extricate yourself from inconvenient, dangerous, or emergency situations as quickly and as expediently as possible.

Expressing a Problem

Out of the clear blue a problem arises. What should you do? What should you say? How can you help others? The terms in Table 14.1 will help you express yourself or help others when something goes wrong unexpectedly.

Table 14.1 Coping with a Problem

English	French	Pronunciation
Calm down!	Calmez-vous!	*kahl-may voo*
Come quickly!	Venez vite!	*vuh-nay veet*
Don't worry!	Ne vous inquiétez pas!	*nuh voo zaN-kee-yeh-tay pah*
Easy does it!	Doucement!	*doos-mahN*
Go away!	Allez-vous-en!	*ah-lay-voo-zahN*
I have a problem!	J'ai un problème!	*zhay uhN proh-blehm*
Help!	Au secours!	*o suh-koor*
Help me!	Aidez-moi!	*eh-day mwah*
Hurry up!	Dépêchez-vous!	*day-peh-shay voo*
It's none of your business!	Ce n'est pas votre affaire!	*suh neh pah vohtr ah-fehr*
Leave me alone!	Laissez-moi tranquille!	*leh-say mwah trahN-keel*
Look! Watch!	Regardez!	*ruh-gahr-day*
Listen!	Écoutez!	*ay-koo-tay*
She (He) is following me.	Elle (Il) me suit.	*ehl (eel) muh swee*
Stop that person!	Arrêtez cette personne.	*ah-reh-tay seht pehr-sohn*
Take it easy!	Ne vous énervez pas!	*nuh voo zay-nehr-vay pah*
Wait!	Espérez!	*ehs-pay-ray*
Watch out!	Attention!	*ah-tahN-syohN*
What's the matter?	Qu'est-ce qu'il y a?	*kehs keel yah*

Getting and Offering Help

You've stated that a problem exists or you've tried to help someone else cope. Now you need assistance or you want to lend a helping hand to someone else. You might even want a translator to help you when you're too upset to speak a foreign language. The phrases that follow should prove invaluable in emergency situations:

Help me, please.
Aidez-moi, s'il vous plaît.
eh-day mwah seel voo pleh

I'm lost.
Je suis perdu(e).   Je me suis égaré(e).
zhuh swee pehr-dew   *zhuh muh swee zay-gah-ray*

I need an interpreter.
Il me faut un interprète.
eel muh fo tuhN naN-tehr-preht

Does anyone here speak English?
Y a-t-il quelqu'un qui parle anglais?
ee ah teel kehl kuhN kee pahrl ahN-gleh

I lost ...
J'ai perdu ...
zhay pehr-dew

my passport.   my wallet.
mon passeport.   mon portefeuille.
mohN pahs-pohr   *mohN pohr-tuh-fuhy*

Someone has stolen …
Quelqu'un a volé …
kehl kuhN ah voh-lay

my purse.	my suitcase.	my watch.
mon sac.	ma valise.	ma montre.
mohN sahk	*mah vah-leez*	*mah mohNtr*

Please call the police.
Appelez la police, s'il vous plaît.
ah-play lah poh-lees seel voo pleh

I'll call the police.
Je vais appeler la police.
zhuh veh zah-play lah poh-lees

I don't understand.
Je ne comprends pas.
shuh nuh kohN-prahN pah

I didn't hear you.
Je ne vous ai pas compris.
zhuh nuh voo zay pah kohN-pree

What did you say?
Qu'est-ce que vous avez dit?
kehs-kuh voo zah-vay dee

Excuse me.
Excusez-moi. (Pardonnez-moi.)
ehk-skew-zay mwah (pah-doh-nay mwah)

Please speak more slowly.
Parlez plus lentement, s'il vous plaît.
pahr-lay plew lahNt-mahN seel voo pleh

Please repeat.
Répétez, s'il vous plaît.
ray-pay-tay seel voo pleh

Attention!

Emergency numbers in France are:

SAMU (Ambulance)	15
Police	17
Pompiers (Fire Station)	18

Getting to the Right Place

Should you need to report a lost or stolen passport, you'll want to be able to locate your consulate to report. Or if your wallet or traveler's checks have been stolen, you'd probably want to file a police report at the nearest station. Maybe you or someone you love will need emergency medical services. The following phrases should help:

Where is …
Où est …
oo eh

the police station?
le commissariat de police?
luh koh-mee-sah-ryah duh poh-lees

the American consulate?
le consulat américain?
luh kohN-sew-lah ah-may-ree-kaN

the American embassy?
l'ambassade américaine?
lahN-bah-sahd ah-may-ree-kehn

the nearest hospital?
l'hôpital le plus proche?
loh-pee-tahl luh plew prohsh

Is it nearby?
Est-ce tout près?
ehs too preh

Is it far?
Est-ce loin?
ehs lwaN

Chapter 15

Grammar in a Flash

In This Chapter

- Nouns and verbs
- Adjectives and adverbs
- Prepositions

So you really want to speak French like a native. Well, you'll be delighted to know that speaking a foreign language doesn't mean that you have to spend hours memorizing pages of rules and translating sentences word for word. That's the way it was done in school years ago. Many of us can remember that drudgery. With today's new communicative approach, however, it's totally unnecessary for foreign language students to walk around armed with a cumbersome French dictionary. Students are now encouraged to use the language and its patterns naturally, the way a native speaker does. To achieve this goal, you need to know some basic grammar.

The Noun's the Thing

Nouns refer to people, places, things, or ideas. Just like in English, nouns can be replaced by pronouns (such as he, she, it, they). Unlike in English, however, all nouns in French have a gender. This means that all nouns have a *sex*. Now that I have your attention I hate to disappoint you. In this case, *sex* refers to the masculine or feminine designation of the noun. In French, all nouns also have a number (singular or plural). Short articles (words that stand for "the" or "a") serve as noun identifiers and usually help to indicate gender and number. Don't be overly concerned by this. Even if you use the incorrect gender or number, you'll still be understood as long as you select the appropriate word.

Gender

Gender, of course, is very obvious if you're speaking about a man or a woman. But it can be a little tricky with all those other nouns that refer to objects. Use the singular noun identifiers in Table 15.1 to express "the" or "a."

Table 15.1   Singular Noun Markers

	Masculine	Feminine
the	le (l') (*luh*)	la (l') (*lah*)
a, an, one	un (*uhN*)	une (*ewn*)

Attention!

The definite articles *le* and *la* become *l'* for words beginning with a vowel or vowel sound (*h, y*). Although it's quite easy to determine the masculine or feminine gender of the noun when *le* or *la* is used, the noun's gender remains a mystery when *l'* (masculine or feminine) is used. To speak properly, you'll have to learn the indefinite article *un* or *une* for any word that begins with a vowel.

Some nouns can be either masculine or feminine depending on whether the speaker is referring to a male or female. Just change the article without changing the spelling of the noun:

un enfant	une enfant
le touriste	la touriste

Some nouns are always only masculine or feminine no matter the sex of the person to whom you are referring:

Always Masculine	Always Feminine
bébé (*bay-bay*)/baby	connaissance (*koh-neh-sahNs*)/acquaintance
dentiste (*dahN-teest*)/dentist	personne (*pehr-sohn*)/person
médecin (*mayd-saN*)/doctor	vedette (*vuh-deht*)/star
professeur (*proh-feh-suhr*)/teacher	victime (*veek-teem*)/victim

Some noun endings can really make the job of determining gender quite easy. Table 15.2 provides a list of endings that will help do this.

Table 15.2   Masculine and Feminine Endings

Masculine Ending	Example	Feminine Ending	Example
-acle	spectacle *spehk-tahkl*	-ade	limonade *lee-moh-nahd*
-age*	garage *gah-rahzh*	-ale	cathédrale *kah-tay-drahl*
-al	animal *ah-nee-mahl*	-ance	chance *shahNs*
-eau**	château *shah-to*	-ence	essence *eh-sahNs*
-et	ticket *tee-keh*	-ette	chaînette *sheh-neht*
-ier	papier *pah-pyay*	-ie	magie *mah-zhee*
-isme	cyclisme *see-kleez-muh*	-ique	boutique *boo-teek*
-ment	changement *shahNzh-mahN*	-oire	histoire *ees-twahr*
		-sion	expression *ehks-preh-syohN*
		-tion	addition *ah-dee-syohN*
		-ure	coiffure *kwah-fewr*

except page (pahzh) (f.); plage (plahzh) (f.) beach
**except eau (o) (f.) water; peau (po) (f.) skin*

A fast and simple way to get the feminine form of some nouns is to add an *e* to the masculine form. This will create a change in the pronunciation of any feminine noun ending in a *consonant* + *e*. For the masculine noun, the final consonant is not pronounced. For the feminine, the consonant must then be pronounced. Another change is that the final nasal sound of a masculine *-in* (*aN*) ending loses its nasality for the feminine ending. These changes are listed in Table 15.3.

Table 15.3   Gender Changes

Le (L'), Un	La (L'), Une
ami (*ah-mee*)/friend	amie (*ah-mee*)/friend
avocat (*ah-vo-kah*)/lawyer	avocate (*ah-vo-kaht*)/lawyer
client (*klee-yahN*)/client	cliente (*klee-yahNt*)/client
cousin (*koo-zaN*)/cousin	cousine (*koo-zeen*)/cousin

Some masculine noun endings (usually referring to professions) very conveniently have a corresponding feminine ending. Most of the feminine endings sound different, as you will notice in Table 15.4.

Table 15.4   More Sex Changes

Masculine/ Feminine Ending	Example
-an	paysan (*peh-ee-zahN*)/peasant
-anne	paysanne (*peh-ee-zahn*)/peasant
-er	épicier (*ay-pee-syay*)/grocer
-ère	épicière (*ay-pee-syehr*)/grocer
-eur	programmeur (*proh-grah-muhr*)/programmer
-euse	programmeuse (*proh-grah-muhz*)/programmer

continues

Table 15.4 More Sex Changes continued

Masculine/ Feminine Ending	Example
-ien	pharmacien (*fahr-mah-syaN*)/pharmacist
-ienne	pharmacienne (fahr-mah-*syehn*)/pharmacist
-on	patron (*pah-trohN*)/boss
-onne	patronne (*pah-trohn*)/boss
-teur	acteur (*ahk-tuhr*)/actor
-trice	actrice (*ahk -trees*)/actress

Don't use the article *un* or *une* before the name of a profession:

Il est dentiste.   Elle est avocate.

Number

If a French noun refers to more than one person, place, thing, or idea, just like in English, it can be made plural. Table 15.5 shows that it is not enough to simply change the noun. The identifying article must be made plural as well.

Table 15.5 Plural Noun Markers

	Masculine	Feminine
the	les	les
some	des	des

As you see, since plural noun markers are used for both feminine and masculine nouns, they do not enable you to determine gender. They indicate only that the speaker is referring to more than one

noun. This means that you must learn each noun
with its singular noun marker.

Plural Nouns

It's really quite easy to form the plural of most
nouns in French. Just add an *unpronounced s* to the
singular form:

le garçon	les garçons
(*luh gahr-sohN*),	(*lay gahr-sohN*),
un garçon	des garçons
(*uhN gahr-sohN*)	(*day gahr-sohN*)
la fille (*lah fee-y*),	les filles (*lay fee-y*),
une fille (*ewn fee-y*)	des filles (*day fee-y*)
l'enfant (*lahN-fahN*),	les enfants (*lay zahN-fahN*),
un enfant	des enfants
(*uhN nahN-fahN*)	(*day zahN-fahN*)

The French also use the letters *s*, *x*, and *z* to make
plurals. What happens if you have a French noun
that ends in one of these letters? Absolutely nothing!

le prix (*luh pree*)/	les prix (*lay pree*)
the price, prize	
le fils (*luh fees*)/	les fils (*lay fees*)
the son	

Common words that end in *s*:

l'autobus	le mois
(*lo-toh-bews*)/bus	(*luh mwah*)/month

le bras (*luh brah*)/
arm

le pays (*luh pay-ee*)/
country

la fois (*lah fwah*)/
time

le repas (*luh ruh-pah*)/
meal

Common words that end in *x:*

la croix (*lah krwah*)/
cross

la voix (*lah vwah*)/
voice

Other Plurals

The letter *x* is used in French to make plurals.

- For nouns ending in *-eau:*

  le bateau (*luh bah-to*)/boat les bateaux

- For nouns ending in *-eu:*

  le cheveu (*luh shuh vuh*)/hair les cheveux

  The exception is *le pneu (luh pnuh)*/tire: *les pneus.*

- For nouns ending in *-al,* change *al* to *aux:*

  l'animal (*lah nee mahl*)/animal les animaux

  Exceptions are le bal (*luh bahl*)/ball: bals; le festival (*luh fehs-tee-vahl*)/festival: festivals.

- For some nouns ending in *-ou,* add *x* to form the plural:

  le bijou (*luh bee-zhoo*)/jewel les bijoux

- Just as we have some words in English that are always plural (pants, sunglasses, shorts, news), so do the French. Here are some nouns that might prove useful to you:

les ciseaux *m.* (*lay see-zo*)/ scissors
les lunettes *f.* (*lay lew-neht*)/eyeglasses
les gens *m.* (*lay zhahN*)/people
les vacances *f.* (*lay vah-kahNs*)/vacation

Verbs Show Action

Verbs indicate an action or a state of being. All verbs must have a subject, whether it is expressed in a statement or implied in a command. The subject can be a noun or pronoun, and, just like in English, it is given a person and a number as shown in Table 15.6.

Table 15.6 Subject Pronouns

Person	Singular		Plural	
first	je* (*zhuh*)	I	nous (*noo*)	we
second	tu** (*tew*)	you	vous** (*voo*)	you
third	il (*eel*)	he, it	ils*** (*eel*)	they
	elle (*ehl*)	she, it	elles (*ehl*)	they
	on (*ohN*)	one, you, we, they		

*The subject pronoun je *requires elision and becomes* j' *before a vowel or vowel sound (*h, y*).*

**The subject pronoun tu *is used when speaking to a single (one) friend, relative, child, or pet.* Tu *is called the familiar form. The* u *from* tu *is never dropped for elision:* tu arrives.

**The subject pronoun vous *is used in the singular to show respect to an older person or when speaking to someone you don't know very well.* Vous *is always used when speaking to more than one person, regardless of familiarity.* Vous *is referred to as the polite form.*

***The subject pronoun ils *is used to refer to more than one male or a combined group of males and females.*

Regular Verbs

Verbs are shown in their infinitive form: *to* live, *to* laugh, *to* love. An infinitive is the form of the verb before it has been conjugated. In a normal English conversation, we conjugate verbs automatically without even paying attention to what we're doing. *Conjugation* refers to changing the ending of a verb so it agrees with the subject. Verbs can be regular (they follow a set pattern of rules) or irregular (there are no rules so you must memorize them).

There are three large families of regular verbs in French: verbs whose infinitives end in *-er*, *-ir*, or *-re*. The verbs within each family are all conjugated in exactly the same manner, so after you've learned the pattern for one family, you know all the verbs in that family. Just drop the underlined infinitive endings and add the conjugated ending that corresponds to the subject:

trouv*er* (to find)	chois*ir* (to choose)	attend*re* (to wait)
je trouv*e*	je chois*is*	j'attend*s*
tu trouv*es*	tu chois*is*	tu attend*s*
il, elle, on trouv*e*	il, elle, on chois*it*	il, elle, on attend
nous trouv*ons*	nous chois*issons*	nous attend*ons*
vous trouv*ez*	vous chois*issez*	vous attend*ez*
ils, elles trouv*ent*	ils, elles chois*issent*	ils, elles attend*ent*

Verb Tables

Tables 15.7, 15.8, and 15.9 provide practical lists of the most frequently used regular verbs in all three families. These are the ones you'll use the most in any given situation:

Table 15.7   Common *-er* Verbs

French	English	French	English
aider *eh-day*	to help	chercher *shehr-shay*	to look for
commencer *koh-mahN-say*	to begin	demander *duh-mahN-day*	to ask
dépenser *day-pahN-say*	to spend (money)	donner *doh-nay*	to give
écouter *ay-koo-tay*	to listen (to)	étudier *ay-tew-dyay*	to study
fermer *fehr-may*	to close	habiter *ah-bee-tay*	to live (in)
jouer *zhoo-ay*	to play	oublier *oo-blee-yay*	to forget
manger *mahN-zhay*	to eat	parler *pahr-lay*	to speak
penser *pahN-say*	to think	préparer *pray-pah-ray*	to prepare
présenter *pray-zahN-tay*	to present, introduce	regarder *ruh-gahr-day*	to look at, watch
rencontrer *rahN-kohN-tray*	to meet	signer *see-nyay*	to sign
téléphoner *tay-lay-foh-nay*	to telephone	travailler *trah-vah-yay*	to work
voyager *vwah-yah-zhay*	to travel		

Table 15.8 Common –*ir* **Verbs**

French	Pronunciation	English
choisir	*shwah-zeer*	to choose
finir	*fee-neer*	to finish
guérir	*gay-reer*	to cure
jouir	*zhoo-eer*	to enjoy
réfléchir	*ray-flay-sheer*	to reflect, think
réussir	*ray-ew-seer*	to succeed

Table 15.9 Common –*re* **Verbs**

French	Pronunciation	English
attendre	*ah-tahNdr*	to wait (for)
descendre	*deh-sahNdr*	to go (come) down
entendre	*ahN-tahNdr*	to hear
perdre	*pehrdr*	to lose
répondre	*ray-pohNdrah*	to answer
vendre	*vahNdr*	to sell

All About Adjectives

Adjectives are used to describe nouns. All French adjectives must agree in number and gender with the nouns they modify. In a French sentence, all words must agree with each other. In other words, if a noun is plural, its adjective must also be plural. And if the noun is feminine, you must be careful to use the feminine form of the adjective.

You can easily form the feminine of most adjectives by adding an *e* to the masculine form as shown in Table 15.10:

Table 15.10 Forming Feminine Adjectives

Masculine	Feminine	Meaning
âgé *ah-zhay*	âgée *ah-zhay*	old, aged
américain *ah-may-ree-kahN*	américaine *ah-may-ree-kehn*	American
amusant *ah-mew-zahN*	amusante *ah-mew-zahNt*	amusing, fun
blond *blohN*	blonde *blohNd*	blond
charmant *shahr-mahN*	charmante *shahr-mahNt*	charming
content *kohN-tahN*	contente *kohN-tahNt*	glad
élégant *ay-lay-gahN*	élégante *ay-lay-gahNt*	elegant
fort *fohr*	forte *fohrt*	strong
français *frahN-seh*	française *frahN-sehz*	French
grand *grahN*	grande *grahNd*	big
intelligent *aN-teh-lee-zhahN*	intelligente *aN-teh-lee-zhahNt*	intelligent
joli *zhoh-lee*	jolie *zhoh-lee*	pretty
petit *puh-tee*	petite *puh-teet*	small
poli *poh-lee*	polie *poh-lee*	polite

When an adjective ends in an *-e* in its masculine form, it is not necessary to make any changes at all to get the feminine form. Both are spelled and pronounced exactly the same:

célèbre (*say-lehbr*)/
famous

mince (*maNs*)/
thin

comique (*koh-meek*)/
comical

propre (*prohpr*/
clean

facile (*fah-seel*)/easy

sale (*sahl*)/dirty

honnête (*oh-neht*)/
honest

triste (*treest*)/
sad

When a masculine adjective ends in -*x*, the feminine is formed by changing *x* to *se*, which gives the feminine ending a *z* sound, as shown in Table 15.11.

Table 15.11   Adjectives Ending in -*eux* and -*euse*

Masculine	Feminine
affectueux *ah-fehk-tew-uh*	affectueuse *ah-fehk-tew-uhz*
ambitieux *ahN-bee-syuh*	ambitieuse *ahN-bee-syuhz*
délicieux *day-lee-syuh*	délicieuse *day-lee-syuhz*
généreux *zhay-nay-ruh*	généreuse *zhay-nay-ruhz*
heureux (happy) *uh-ruh*	heureuse *uh-ruhz*
sérieux *say-ryuh*	sérieuse *say-ryuhz*

When a masculine adjective ends in -*f*, the feminine is formed by changing *f* to *ve*. See Table 15.12 for pronunciation changes.

Table 15.12   Adjectives Ending in -*f* and -*ve*

Masculine	Feminine
actif	active
ahk-teef	*ahk-teev*
attentif	attentive
ah-tahN-teef	*ah-tahN-teev*
imaginatif	imaginative
ee-mah-zhee-nah-teef	*ee-mah-zhee-nah-teev*
naïf	naïve
nah-eef	*nah-eev*
sportif	sportive
spohr-teef	*spohr-teev*

When a masculine adjective ends in *er*, the feminine is formed by changing *er* to *ère*, as shown in Table 15.13:

Table 15.13   Adjectives Ending in -*er* and -*ère*

Masculine	Feminine	Meaning
cher	chère	dear, expensive
shehr	*shehr*	
dernier	dernière	last
dehr-nyay	*dehr-nyehr*	
étranger	étrangère	foreign
ay-trahN-zhay	*ay-trahN-zhehr*	
fier	fière	proud
fyehr	*fyehr*	
premier	première	first
pruh-myay	*puh-myehr*	

Some masculine adjectives double the final consonant and then add *e* to form the feminine, as shown in Table 15.14.

Table 15.14 Adjectives that Double Their Consonants

Masculine	Feminine	Meaning
ancien *ahN-syaN*	ancienne *ahN-syehn*	ancient, old
bas *bah*	basse *bahs*	low
bon *bohN*	bonne *bohn*	good
européen *ew-roh-pay-aN*	européenne *ew-roh-pay-ehn*	European
gentil *zhahN-tee-y*	gentille *zhahN-tee-y*	nice, kind
gros *gro*	grosse *gros*	fat, big
mignon *mee-nyohN*	mignonne *mee-noyhn*	cute

Finally, the adjectives in Table 15.15 list irregular feminine forms that must be memorized.

Table 15.15 Irregular Adjectives

Masculine	Feminine	Meaning
beau* *bo*	belle *behl*	beautiful
blanc *blahN*	blanche *blahNsh*	white
complet *kohN-pleh*	complète *kohN-pleht*	complete
doux *doo*	douce *doos*	sweet, gentle
faux *fo*	fausse *fos*	false
favori *fah-voh-ree*	favorite *fah-voh-reet*	favorite
frais *freh*	fraîche *frehsh*	fresh

Masculine	Feminine	Meaning
long *lohN*	longue *lohNg*	long
nouveau* *noo-vo*	nouvelle *noo-vehl*	new
vieux* *vyuh*	vieille *vyay*	old

*The French use special forms: bel, nouvel, *and* vieil **before** masculine nouns beginning with a vowel or vowel sound to prevent a clash between two pronounced vowel sounds. This allows the language to flow.*

> *un bel appartement   un nouvel appartement*
> *un vieil appartement*

*If the adjective comes **after** the noun, then the regular masculine form is used:*

L'appartement est beau.
L'appartement est nouveau.
L'appartement est vieux.

Making Adjectives Plural

Most adjectives are made plural by adding an unpronounced *s* to the singular form: *timide(s), charmant(e)s, joli(e)s, fatigué(e)s*.

If an adjective ends in -*s* or -*x*, it is unnecessary to add the *s*: *exquis, heureux*.

Most masculine singular adjectives ending in -*al* change *al* to *aux* in the plural: *spéciaux*.

The special masculine singular adjectives *bel, nouvel,* and *vieil* do not need special plural forms, since the problem of having two conflicting vowels is eliminated with the *x* consonant sound of the plural ending.

Singular	Plural	Example
bel	beaux	de beaux appartements
nouvel	nouveaux	de nouveaux appartements
vieil	vieux	de vieux appartements

The masculine singular adjective tout *(all) becomes* tous *in the plural.*

The Position of Adjectives

In French, most adjectives are placed after the nouns they modify. Compare this with English, where we do the opposite:

un homme intéressant   an interesting man

Adjectives showing …

BEAUTY: beau, joli
AGE: jeune, nouveau, vieux
GOODNESS (or lack of it): bon, gentil, mauvais, villain
SIZE: grand, petit, court, long, gros, large

generally go before the nouns they modify. Remember **BAGS,** and you'll have no trouble with these adjectives:

un beau garçon   a handsome boy
une large avenue   a wide avenue

If more than one adjective is being used in a description, put each adjective in its proper position:

une bonne histoire intéressante

une large et jolie avenue

un homme charmant et intelligent

Using Adverbs

Adverbs are words that describe verbs, adjectives, or other adverbs. In English, most adverbs end in *-ly:* for example, He dances slowly. In French, however, they end in *-ment:* for example, *Il danse lentement.* Adverbs shouldn't pose many problems as you learn the language.

Add *ment* to the masculine, singular form of adjectives that end in a vowel. If the masculine form of the adjective ends in a consonant, first change it to the feminine form and then add *ment*.

How to form adverbs using masculine adjectives:

Adjective	Adverb	Meaning
passionné	passionnément	enthusiastically
pah-syoh-nay	*pah-syoh-nay-mahN*	
rapide	rapidement	rapidly, quickly
rah-peed	*rah-peed-mahN*	
vrai	vraiment	truly, really
vreh	*vreh-mahN*	

How to form adverbs from feminine adjectives:

Adjective	Adverb	Meaning
active *ahk-teev*	activement *ahk-teev-mahN*	actively
complète *kohN-pleht*	complètement *kohN-pleht-mahN*	completely
continuelle *kohN-tee-new-ehl*	continuellement *kohN-tee-new-ehl-mahN*	continuously
douce *doos*	doucement *doos-mahN*	gently
fière *fyehr*	fièrement *fyehr-mahN*	proudly
franche *frahNsh*	franchement *frahNsh-mahN*	frankly
lente *lahNt*	lentement *lahNt-mahN*	slowly
sérieuse *say-ree-uhz*	sérieusement *say-ree-uhz-mahN*	seriously
seule *suhl*	seulement *suhl-mahN*	only

Exceptions to the Rule

Wouldn't life be so easy if there were no exceptions to the rules? Fortunately, the irregularities in French adverbs are easy to understand and should present no difficulties.

Some adverbs are formed by changing a silent *e* from the adjective to *é* before the adverbial *-ment* ending:

Adjective	Adverb	Meaning
énorme *ay-nohrm*	énormément *ay-nohr-may-mahN*	enormously
profond *proh-fohN*	profondément *proh-fohN-day-mahN*	profoundly

Adjectives ending in *-ant* and *-ent* have adverbs ending in *-amment* and *-emment*, respectively:

Adjective	Adverb	Meaning
constant *kohN-stahN*	constamment *kohN-stah-mahN*	constantly
courant *koo-rahN*	couramment *koo-rah-mahN*	fluently
évident *ay-vee-dahN*	évidemment *ay-vee-deh-mahN*	evidently
récent *ray-sahN*	récemment *ray-seh-mahN*	recently

Be careful with these adverbs, which have distinct forms from adjectives:

Adjective	Adverb
bon (*bohN*)/good	bien (*byaN*)/well
mauvais (*moh-veh*)/bad	mal (*mahl*)/badly
meilleur (*meh-yuhr*)/better	mieux (*myuh*)/better
petit (*puh-tee*)/little	peu (*puh*)/little

If you can't think of the adverb, or if one does not exist, use the phrases *d'une façon* (*dewn fah-sohN*) or *d'une manière* (*dewn mah-nyehr*), which both express *in a way*, *in a manner*, or *in a fashion*.

He plays intelligently.
Il joue d'une façon (d'une manière) intelligente.

Some adverbs and adverbial expressions are not formed from adjectives at all and therefore, do not end in *-ment*. Table 15.16 gives the most common adverbs that follow this rule. These familiar, high-frequency words are extremely useful in everyday conversation.

Table 15.16   Adverbs Not Formed from Adjectives

French	English	French	English
alors *ah-lohrs*	then	après *ah-preh*	afterward
aussi *o-see*	also, too	beaucoup *bo-koo*	much
bientôt *byaN-to*	soon	comme *kohm*	as
d'habitude *dah-bee-tewd*	usually, generally	déjà *day-zhah*	already
encore *ahN-kohr*	still, yet, again	ensemble *ahN-sahNbl*	together
maintenant *maNt-nahN*	now	moins *mwaN*	less
plus *plew*	more	quelquefois *kehl-kuh-fwah*	sometimes
souvent *soo-vahN*	often	tard *tahr*	late
tôt *to*	soon, early	toujours *too-zhoor*	always, still
tout *too*	quite, entirely	très *treh*	very
trop *tro*	too much	vite *veet*	quickly

Position of Adverbs

Adverbs are generally placed after the verb they modify. Sometimes, however, the position of the adverb is variable and is usually placed where we would logically put an English adverb.

> D'habitude il joue bien au football.
> Il joue très bien au football.

Prepositions

Prepositions show the relationship between a noun and another word in a sentence. Table 15.17 shows common prepositions you will find useful:

Table 15.17   Prepositions

French	English	French	English
à *ah*	to, at	après *ah-preh*	after
avant *ah-vahN*	before	chez *shay*	at the house (business) of
contre *kohNtr*	against	dans *dahN*	in
de *duh*	from	derrière *deh-ryehr*	behind
devant *duh-vahN*	in front of	en *ahN*	in
entre *ahNtr*	between	loin (de) *lwaN (duh)*	far (from)
par *pahr*	by, through	pour *poor*	for, in order to
près (de) *preh (duh)*	near	sans *sahN*	without

continues

Table 15.17 Prepositions continued

French	English	French	English
sous *soo*	under	sur *sewr*	on
vers *vehr*	toward		

The following pronouns are used after prepositions:

moi	me	nous	us
toi	you	vous	you
lui	him	eux	them *m.*
elle	her	elles	them *f.*

Verbs in a Flash

In This Chapter

- The present
- The passé composé and the imperfect
- The future and the conditional
- The subjunctive

All sentences must have a verb. Are you aware that a command is probably the simplest sentence of all and may consist of only one word, a verb, for example: Go!

Our very full, active lives require that we use verbs in a specific tense or time frame: past, present, or future. We also have a choice of moods: the indicative (states a fact in the past, present, or future tense); the imperative or command form; the conditional (states what a subject would do under certain conditions); or the subjunctive (expresses wishing, emotion, doubt, need, or necessity in the past, present, or future). In order to communicate exactly what you want to say it is important to have a complete understanding of tenses and moods.

The Present

The present tense is used ...

- To express what is happening or does happen now:

  Les garçons jouent au football.
  The boys are playing (do play) soccer.

- To express what generally happens in the present:

  Je regarde la télévision à dix heures le soir.
  I watch television at 10 o'clock at night.

- To imply the immediate future or to ask for instructions:

  Je te parle demain.
  I'll speak to you tomorrow.

  Je fais cela?
  Shall I do that?

- With *depuis* + an expression of time to express an action or event that began in the past and that is continuing in the present. The question is expressed by *Depuis combien de temps* ... + present tense, or *Depuis quand* ... + present tense:

  Depuis combien de temps est-ce que vous habitez ici?
  Depuis quand est-ce que vous habitez ici?
  How long (Since when) have you been living here?

  J'habite ici depuis deux ans.
  I've been living here for two years.

- With *il y a* + time + *que* + present to express an action or event that began in the past and that is continuing in the present. The question is expressed by *Combien de temps y a-t-il que* ... + present tense:

  Combien de temps y a-t-il que vous habitez ici?
  How long have you been living here?

  Il y a deux ans que j'habite ici.
  I've been living here for two years.

Attention!

Verbs ending in *−er, -ir,* and *−re* are regular verbs and all verbs in those families follow the same rules for present tense conjugation. Verbs that have irregular present tense conjugations can be found in Appendix A. They are generally very high-frequency verbs and must be memorized.

"Shoe verbs" require a spelling change that works as if we put the subject pronouns that follow one set of rules within the shoe and the others outside the shoe. The shoe looks like this:

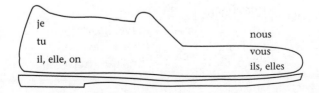

je
tu
il, elle, on

nous
vous
ils, elles

Note that these verbs have changes for all subject pronouns except *nous*.

The changes occur as follows:

- Verbs ending in –*cer* change *c* to *ç* before *o* to retain the soft *c* sound:

  commen**c**er (to begin)
  je commence
  nous commen**ç**ons

- Verbs ending in –*ger* insert a silent *e* between *g* and *o* to keep the soft *g* sound:

  man**g**er (to eat)
  je mange
  nous mang**e**ons

For the following verbs, the shoe has a smaller toe and there are changes for all subject pronouns except *nous* and *vous*:

je	nous
tu	vous
il, elle, on	ils, elles

- Verbs ending in –*yer* change *y* to *i* before silent *e*. Note that for verbs ending in –*ayer* this change is optional:

  envo**y**er (to send)   **pay**er (to pay)
  j'envo**i**e   je pa**i**e (je pa**y**e)
  tu envo**i**es   tu pa**i**es (tu pa**y**es)

il envo*i*e   il paie (il paye)
nous envoyons   nous payons
vous envoyez   vous payez
ils envo*i*ent   ils paient (ils payent)

- Verbs ending in *e* + consonant + *er* change
  the silent *e* to *è* in all forms except *nous* and
  vous. Note that the verbs *appeler* and *jeter*
  double their final consonant instead of
  adding the accent mark:

acheter	appeler	jeter
(to buy)	(to call)	(to throw)
j'ach**è**te	j'appe**ll**e	je je**tt**e
tu ach**è**tes	tu appe**ll**es	tu je**tt**es
il ach**è**te	il appe**ll**e	il je**tt**e
nous achetons	nous appelons	nous jetons
vous achetez	vous appelez	vous jetez
ils ach**è**tent	ils appe**ll**ent	ils je**tt**ent

- Verbs with *é* in the syllable before the *-er*
  infinitive ending change *é* to *è* in all forms
  except *nous* and *vous*:

préférer (to prefer)
je préf**è**re
tu préf**è**res
il préf**è**re
nous préférons
vous préférez
ils préf**è**rent

The Passé Composé (The Compound Past)

The *passé composé* expresses an action or event that was begun or completed at a specific time in the past, even if the time isn't mentioned:

> Le concert a commencé a huit heures.
> The concert began at eight o'clock.

> Je me suis couché(e) de bonne heure.
> I went to bed early.

The *passé composé* may also express an action or event that was repeated a stated number of times.

> J'ai vu ce film trois fois.
> I saw that film three times.

The compound past is composed of two parts: the helping verb and the past participle.

The helping verb expresses that an action "has" taken place. In most instances, the French use the verb *avoir* (to have) as the helping verb. Verbs of motion (those showing action that indicates a change) use *être* as their helping verb.

Helping verbs are conjugated in their present tense forms:

	avoir	être
je (j')	ai	suis
tu	as	es
il/elle	a	est

nous	avons	sommes
vous	avez	êtes
ils/elles	ont	sont

The past participle expresses the action that "happened." The past participle is added after the conjugated helping verb. To form the past participle of regular verbs, drop the infinitive ending (-*er*, -*ir*, -*re*) and add the endings as illustrated in Table 16.1.

Table 16.1   Forming the Passé Composé of Regular Verbs

-*er* verbs	-*ir* verbs	-*re* verbs
danser (to dance)	finir (to finish)	perdre (to lose)
dans**é**	fin**i**	perd**u**

Ils ont dansé.	They danced.
J'ai fini mon travail.	I finished my work.
Elle a perdu sa clef.	She lost her key.

The passé composé of irregular verbs is formed by adding an irregular past participle to the conjugated helping verb. Although irregular verbs also have irregular past participles, they can be grouped according to their endings, in most cases:

- Past participles ending in -*u*:

avoir	eu	had
boire	bu	drank
connaître	connu	known, knew
croire	cru	believed
devoir	dû	had to, owed
lire	lu	read

pleuvoir	plu	rained
pouvoir	pu	was able to
recevoir	reçu	received
savoir	su	knew
voir	vu	seen, saw
vouloir	voulu	wanted

● Past participles ending in *-is*:

mettre	mis	put (on)
prendre	pris	took

● Past participles ending in *-it*:

conduire	conduit	driven, drove
dire	dit	said, told
écrire	écrit	written, wrote

● Irregular past participles:

être	été	been, was
faire	fait	made, done, did
offrir	offert	offered
ouvrir	ouvert	opened

J'ai fait un voyage.　　　I took a trip.

If an irregular verb is contained within a larger verb, both generally form their past participles in the same way: *mettre—mis; promettre—promis; ouvrir—ouvert; découvrir—découvert.*

Some verbs use *être* as their helping verb. These verbs form the mnemonic DR and MRS VANDERTRAMPP, as shown in Table 16.2. An * indicates an irregular past participle.

Table 16.2   Verbs Requiring *être* as Their Helping Verb

Infinitive	Past Participle	Meaning
devenir	devenu*	to become
revenir	revenu*	to return
mourir	mort*	to die
retourner	retourné	to return
sortir	sorti	to go out
venir	venu*	to come
arriver	arrivé	to arrive
naître	né*	to be born
descendre	descendu	to go down
entrer	entré	to enter
rentrer	rentré	to return
tomber	tombé	to fall
rester	resté	to remain
aller	allé	to go
monter	monté	to go up
passer	passé	to pass by
partir	parti	to leave

The passé composé is formed by conjugating the helping verb and adding the past participle. When *avoir* is the helping verb, the past participle generally remains constant:

J'ai fait un voyage.	I took a trip.
Elles ont fait un voyage.	They took a trip.

When être, however, is the helping verb, the past participle must agree in number (singular or plural [add *s*]) and gender (masculine or feminine [add *e*]) with the subject, as shown in Table 16.3. Note how the past participle differs with different subjects.

Table 16.3 Forming the Passé Composé with *être*

Masculine Subjects	Feminine Subjects	Meaning
je suis venu	je suis venue	I (have) arrived
tu es venu	tu es venue	you (have) arrived
il est venu	elle est venue	he/she (has) arrived
nous sommes venus	nous sommes venues	we (have) arrived
vous êtes venu(s)	vous êtes venue(s)	you (have) arrived
ils sont venus	elles sont venues	they (have) arrived

Note the following about the passé composé:

- Note that *vous* can be a singular or plural subject for both masculine and feminine subjects.

Singular	**Plural**
Vous êtes sorti.	Vous êtes sortis.
Vous êtes sortie.	Vous êtes sorties.

- For a mixed group, always use the masculine form.

  Roger et Bernard sont montés.
  Lucienne et Marie sont montées.
  Roger et Marie sont montés.

The Imperfect

The imperfect expresses continuous or repeated actions, events, situations, or states in the past and is used …

- To describe what *was* or *used to* happen again and again in the past:

Je lisais un livre.
I was reading a book.

Le samedi elle faisait le ménage.
On Saturdays, she used to (would) do housework.

● To express an ongoing past action:

Il regardais la télé le soir.
He watched television at night.

● To describe people, things, or time in the past:

Ils étaient très polis.
They were very polite.

La porte était ouverte.
The door was open.

C'était mardi.
It was Tuesday.

● To express a state of mind in the past with verbs such as *croire* (to believe), *penser* (to think), *pouvoir* (to be able), *vouloir* (to want), and *savoir* (to know):

Elle voulait faire de son mieux.
She wanted to do her best.

● To describe a situation that was going on when another action occurred:

Je sortais quand mon ami m'a téléphoné.
I was going out when my friend called.

To form the imperfect of regular verbs, drop the *–ons* ending from the present tense *nous* form of the verb and add these endings:

je	-ais	nous	-ions
tu	-ais	vous	-iez
il	-ait	ils	-aient

The only irregular verb in the imperfect is *être*:

j'étais	nous étions
tu étais	vous étiez
il était	ils étaient

The Future

The future can be expressed in three ways:

- By using the present to imply the future:

  Je te vois plus tard.
  I'll see you later.

- By using aller (to go) + the infinitive of a verb:

  Ils vont faire du cyclisme.
  They are going to go cycling.

- By using the future tense:

  Visiteras-tu la France?
  Are you going to visit France?

The future tense is formed by adding the future endings to the infinitive of regular verbs as follows:

je	-ai	nous	-ons
tu	-as	vous	-ez
il	-a	ils	-ont

Je ne travaillerai pas demain.
I'm not going to work tomorrow.

Il réfléchira avant d'agir.
He will think before acting.

Nous vendrons notre maison cette année.
We will sell our house this year.

The following verbs have irregular stems in the future and, therefore, do not use the infinitive. To form the future, simply add the ending to the stems indicated:

aller (to go)	ir-
avoir (to have)	aur-
courir (to run)	courr-
devoir (to have to, owe)	devr-
envoyer (to send)	enverr-
être (to be)	ser-
faire (to do)	fer-
falloir (to be necessary)	faudr-
mourir (to die)	mourr-
pleuvoir (to rain)	pleuvr-
pouvoir (to be able to)	pourr-
recevoir (to receive)	recevr-
savoir (to know)	saur-
venir (to come)	viendr-
voir (to see)	verr-
vouloir (to want)	voudr-

The Conditional

The conditional is a mood that expresses what the subject **would** do or what **would** happen under certain circumstances.

The conditional is formed by adding the imperfect endings to the future stem of regular and irregular verbs as follows:

je	-ais	nous	-ions
tu	-ais	vous	-iez
il	-ait	ils	-aient

M'aideriez-vous?
Would you help me?

Pourrais-je vous parler?
Could I speak to you?

The Subjunctive

The subjunctive is a mood that expresses wishing, wanting, emotion, doubt, and uncertainty. Since the subjunctive is not a tense (a verb form indicating time), the present subjunctive is used to express actions in the present or future.

The subjunctive is used when the following conditions are met:

- There are two different clauses with two different subjects.
- The two clauses are joined by *que*.
- One of the clauses shows wishing, wanting, emotion, doubt, or uncertainty.

To form the subjunctive of regular verbs, drop the
–*ent* ending from the *ils (elles)* form of the present
and add these endings:

je	-e	nous	-ions
tu	-es	vous	-iez
il	-e	ils	-ent

Il est important que nous cherchions ce livre.
It is important that we look for that book.

Je doute qu'il trahisse son ami.
I doubt he will betray his friend.

Il est possible qu'il vende sa voiture.
It is possible that he will sell his car.

Shoe verbs and verbs that are conjugated like shoe
verbs have two different stems in the subjunctive:
One stem is for the *je, tu, il,* and *ils* forms while the
other is for the *nous* and *vous* forms:

boire (to drink)	que je boive	que nous buvions
prendre (to take)	que je prenne	que nous prenions
envoyer (to send)	que j'envoie	que nous envoyions
acheter (to buy)	que j'achète	que nous achetions
appeler (to call)	que j'appelle	que nous appelions

| jeter (to throw) | que je jette | que nous jetions |
| répéter (to repeat) | que je répète | que nous répétions |

High-frequency irregular verbs used in the sub-junctive include:

aller (to go): aille, ailles, aille, allions, alliez, aillent

vouloir (to want): veuille, veuille, veuille, voulions, vouliez, veuillent

faire (to make, do): fasse, fasses, fasse, fassions, fassiez, fassent

pouvoir (to be able to): puisse, puisses, puisse, puissions, puissiez, puissent

savoir (to know): sache, saches, sache, sachions, sachiez, sachent

avoir (to have): aie, aies, ait, ayons, ayez, aient

être (to be): sois, sois, soit, soyons, soyez, soient

Idioms in a Flash

In This Chapter

- Idiomatically speaking
- Verbal idioms
- Miscellaneous idioms
- Bordering on slang

Are you aware that all languages contain idiomatic expressions? An idiom is a particular word or expression whose meaning cannot be readily understood by either its grammar or the words used to express it. Although idioms may seem illogical, they allow you to speak and express yourself in a foreign language the way a native speaker would. Idioms are perfectly acceptable patterns belonging to the standard vocabulary of the language and they are listed in bilingual dictionaries.

Speaking Idiomatically

Want a better understanding of idioms? Take a quick glance at some common English idioms that would probably confuse a foreign speaker trying to use the language. It is very easy to see why a word-by-word translation of these sentences might cause quite a bit of confusion:

> You're driving me crazy!

> I have some time to kill.

> It's raining cats and dogs.

> You'll have to pay through the nose.

An Extra Workout _____

Keep handy a list of the idioms you learn in each chapter. Try to use the ones that will be most helpful to you in situations in which you will speak the language.

Verbal Idioms

Some idioms are formed with verbs. To use them, simply conjugate the verb to agree with the subject. Make sure that you put the verb in the proper tense (past, present, future) or mood (conditional, subjunctive).

Attention! _____

Faire is used to describe the weather while _avoir_ is used to describe the physical condition of a person:

Il fait chaud.   The weather is hot.

J'ai chaud.   I'm hot.

apprendre par coeur *ah-prahNdr pahr kuhr*	to memorize
avoir ... ans *ah-vwahr ... ahN*	to be ... years old
avoir besoin de *ah-vwahr buh-zwaN duh*	to need
avoir chaud *ah-vwahr sho*	to be warm (of persons)
avoir envie de *ah-vwahr ahN-vee duh*	to feel like
avoir faim *ah-vwahr faN*	to be hungry
avoir froid *ah-vwahr frwah*	to be cold (of persons)
avoir lieu *ah-vwahr lyuh*	to take place
avoir mal (à + body part) *ah-vwahr mahl (ah)*	to have a pain (in), have a(an) ache
avoir peur (de) *ah-vwahr puhr (duh)*	to be afraid of
avoir raison *ah-vwahr reh-zohN*	to be right
avoir soif *ah-vwahr swahf*	to be thirsty
avoir tort *ah-vwahr tohr*	to be wrong
avoir de la chance *ah-vwahr duh lah shahNs*	to be lucky

avoir l'habitude de *ah-vwahr lah-bee-tood duh*	to be accustomed to
avoir l'intention de *ah-vwahr laN-tahN- syohN duh*	to intend to
avoir l'occasion de *ah-vwahr loh-kah-zyohN duh*	to have the opportunity to
avoir le temps de *ah-vwahr luh tahn duh*	to have (the) time to
donner sur *doh-nay sewr*	to face, look out on
être à *ehtr ah*	to belong to
être d'accord (avec) *ehtr dah-kohr (ah-vehk)*	to agree (with)
être en train de *ehtr ahN traN duh*	to be busy (doing something)
être sur le point de *ehtr sewr luh pwaN duh*	to be about to
y être *ee ehtr*	to understand, see the point
faire beau *fehr bo*	to be nice weather
faire chaud *fehr cho*	to be hot weather
faire du vent *fehr dew vahN*	to be windy

faire frais *fehr freh*	to be cool weather
faire froid *fehr frwah*	to be cold weather
faire mauvais *feh mo-veh*	to be bad weather
faire attention à *fehr ah-tahN-syohN ah*	to pay attention to
faire des achats *fehr day zah-shah*	to go shopping
faire la connaissance de *fehr lah koh-neh-sahNs duh*	to become acquainted with
faire une partie de *fehr ewn pahr-tee duh*	to play a game of
faire une promenade *fehr ewn prohm-nahd*	to take a walk, a ride
faire un voyage *fehr uhN vwah-yahzh*	to take a trip
n'en pouvoir plus *nahN poo-vwahr plew*	to be exhausted
valoir la peine (de + inf.) *vah-lwahr lah pehn (duh)*	to be worthwhile
valoir mieux *vah-lwahr myuh*	to be better
venir de *vuh-neer duh*	to have just (in present and imperfect)
vouloir dire *voo-lwahr deer*	to mean

Here are some examples showing you how to use these idioms. Note how different subjects, tenses, and moods can be used:

> Je n'en peux plus.
> I'm exhausted.

> Qu'est-ce que ça veut dire?
> What does that mean?

> Ils venaient d'arriver.
> They had just arrived.

> Il faut que tu fasses attention.
> It is necessary that you pay attention.

Miscellaneous Idiomatic Expressions

Some idiomatic expressions begin with prepositions and refer to time, travel, location, and direction. Others enable you to express your feelings and opinions about things. The following list provides common idioms that should come in quite handy.

à (with time expressions) *ah*	good-bye, until
à demain *ah duh-maN*	see you tomorrow
à jamais *ah zhah-meh*	forever
à l'heure *ah luhr*	on time

à partir de
ah pahr-teer duh

from … on, beginning (with)

à peu près
ah puh preh

nearly, about, approximately

à propos de, au sujet de
ah proh-po

about, concerning

à quoi bon (+ infinitive)?
ah kwah bohN

what's the use of?

à tout à l'heure
ah too tah luhr

see you in a little while

au contraire
o kohN-trehr

on the contrary

au revoir
o ruh-vwahr

good-bye, see you again

bien entendu, bien sûr
*byaN nahN-tahN-dew,
byaN sewr*

of course

bon marché
bohN mahr-shay

cheap

C'est entendu.
seh tahN-tahN-dew

It's agreed. All right.

c'est-à-dire
seh tah deer

that is to say

Cela m'est égal.
suh-lah meh tay-gahl

It makes no difference to me. That's all the same to me.

Cela ne fait rien.
suh-lah nuh feh ryaN

That doesn't matter. It makes no difference.

d'abord
dah-bohr

first, at first

D'accord.
dah-kohr

Agreed. Okay.

de bonne heure
duh boh nuhr

early

de la part de
duh lah pahr duh

on behalf of, from

de nouveau
duh noo-vo

again

de quelle couleur ...?
duh kehl koo-luhr

what color ...?

De rien.
duh ryaN

You're welcome.

Il n'y a pas de quoi.
eel nyah pah duh kwah

Don't mention it.

en effet
ahN neh-feh

(yes) indeed, as a
matter of fact

en même temps
ahN mehm tahN

at the same time

en retard
ahN ruh-tahr

late (= not on time)

en tout cas
ahN too kah

in any case, at any
rate

en ville
ahN veel

downtown, in (to,
into) town

encore une fois
ahN-kohr ewn fwah

again

et ainsi de suite *ay aN-see duh sweet*	and so forth
grâce à *grahs ah*	thanks to
il y a + time *eel yah*	ago
meilleur marché *meh-yuhr mahr-shay*	cheaper
n'importe *naN-pohrt*	never mind, no matter
par conséquent *pahr kohN-say-kahN*	therefore, consequently
par exemple *pahr ehg-zahNpl*	for example
par hasard *pahr ah-zahr*	by chance
peu à peu *puh ah puh*	little by little, gradually
peut-être *puh tehtr*	perhaps, maybe
quant à *kahN tah*	as for
quel *kehl*	what, what a
sans doute *sahN doot*	without a doubt
s'il vous plaît *seel voo pleh*	please

tant mieux *tahN myuh*	so much the better
tant pis *tahN pee*	so much the worse, too bad
tous (les) deux *too (lay) duh*	both
tout à (d'un) coup *too tah (duhN) koo*	suddenly
tout à fait *too tah feh*	entirely, quite
tout de même *tood mehm*	all the same
tout de suite *toot sweet*	immediately
tout le monde *too luh mohNd*	everybody

Here are some examples using these idioms:

Au revoir. À demain.
Good-bye. See you tomorrow.

Je le répéterai encore une fois.
I'll repeat it again.

Il parle de la part de son frère.
He speaks on behalf of his brother.

Je te rappelle tout de suite.
I'll call you back immediately.

An Extra Workout

Use "quel ...!" to express "what" or "what a." Quel (quelle, quels, quelles) must agree in number and gender with the noun it modifies:

Quel désastre!
What a disaster!
Quels bons desserts!
What good desserts!
Quelle chance!
What luck!
Quelles femmes charmantes!
What charming women!

Almost Slang

What constitutes slang? Colorful, popular, informal words or expressions that are not part of the standard vocabulary of the language are considered slang. Slang, also known as street language, is deemed unconventional, but certainly contributes a degree of variety and interest to any language. The following phrases may be considered mild slang and may come in handy one day:

Big deal!	Tu parles!
	tew pahrl
Cut it out!	Ça suffit!
	sah sew-fee

Get out of here!	Va-t'en! *vah-tahN*
Good riddance!	Bon débarras! *bohN day-bah-rah*
I can't get over it!	Je n'en reviens pas! *zhuh nahN ruh-vyaN pah*
I'm really fed up!	Ras le bol! *rah luh bohl*
I've had it up to here!	J'en ai marre! *zhahN nay mahr*
It goes without saying.	Il va sans dire. *eel vah sahN deer*
It's a pleasure.	Je vous en prie. *zhuh voo zahN pree*
It's not worth it.	Ça ne vaut pas la peine. *sah nuh vo pah lah pehn*
Keep your shirt on!	Reste couvert! *rehst koo-vehr*
Knock it off!	Assez de bêtises! *ah-say duh beh-teez*
Leave me alone!	Laisse–moi tranquille! *lehs-mwah trahN-keel*
Make up your mind!	Décide-toi! *day-seed-twah*
Mind your own business!	Mêle-toi de tes affaires! *mehl-twah duh tay zah-fehr*

Never mind!	N'importe. *naN-pohrt*
No kidding?	Sans blague? *sahN blahg*
No way!	Pas question! *pah kehs-tyohN*
Of course!	Bien sûr! *byaN sewr*
Oh no!	Mais non! *meh nohN*
Shame on you!	Honte à toi! *ohN tah twah*
Thank heavens!	Grâce au ciel! *grahs o syehl*
That bugs me!	Ça m'inquiète! *sah maN-kee-yeht*
That infuriates me!	Ça me fait rager! *sah me feh rah-zhay*
That's going too far!	Cela dépasse les bornes! *suh-lah day-pahs lay bohrn*
That's the last straw!	Ça, c'est le comble! *sah seh luh kohNbl*
There's no doubt.	Il n'y a pas de doute. *eel nyah pah duh doot*
Wow!	Oh là là! *oh lah lah*
You bet!	Un peu! *uhN puh*

You can say that again!	C'est le cas de le dire! *seh luh kah duh luh deer*
You must be kidding!	Tu parles! *tew pahrl*
You're driving me nuts!	Tu me rends fou (folle)! *tew muh rahN foo (fohl)*
You're too much!	C'est trop fort! *seh tro fohr*

Attention! _____

Idiomatic and slang expressions exist is all languages. For that reason, it's impossible to do a word-for-word translation from one language to the next. For best results, simply try to think of the phrase you want in the language you want.

Verb Charts

Regular Verbs

-*er* Verbs

PARLER   to speak
Past participle: parl*é*; Commands: Parle! Parlez!

Subj.	Present (is)	Imperfect (was)	Future (will)	Conditional (would)
je	parl*e*	parl*ais*	parler*ai*	parler*ais*
tu	parl*es*	parl*ais*	parler*as*	parler*ais*
il	parl*e*	parl*ait*	parler*a*	parler*ait*
nous	parl*ons*	parl*ions*	parler*ons*	parler*ions*
vous	parl*ez*	parl*iez*	parler*ez*	parler*iez*
ils	parl*ent*	parl*aient*	parler*ont*	parler*aient*

-ir Verbs

FINIR to finish

Past participle: fin*i;* Commands: Finis! Finissez!

Subj.	Present (is)	Imperfect (was)	Future (will)	Conditional (would)
je	fin*is*	finiss*ais*	finir*ai*	finir*ais*
tu	fin*is*	finiss*ais*	finir*as*	finir*ais*
il	fin*it*	finiss*ait*	finir*a*	finir*ait*
nous	fin*issons*	finiss*ions*	finir*ons*	finir*ions*
vous	fin*issez*	finiss*iez*	finir*ez*	finir*iez*
ils	fin*issent*	finiss*aient*	finir*ont*	finir*aient*

-re Verbs

VENDRE to sell

Past participle: vend*u;* Commands: Vends! Vendez!

Subj.	Present (is)	Imperfect (was)	Future (will)	Conditional (would)
je	vend*s*	vend*ais*	vendr*ai*	vendr*ais*
tu	vend*s*	vend*ais*	vendr*as*	vendr*ais*
il	vend	vend*ait*	vendr*a*	vendr*ait*
nous	vend*ons*	vend*ions*	vendr*ons*	vendr*ions*
vous	vend*ez*	vend*iez*	vendr*ez*	vendr*iez*
ils	vend*ent*	vend*aient*	vendr*ont*	vendr*aient*

Irregular Verbs

*Verbs conjugated with être in the past tense are indicated by a *.

ALLER   to go *
Past participle: all*é*; Commands: Va! Allez!

Subj.	Present	Subj.	Present
je	vais	nous	allons
tu	vas	vous	allez
il	va	ils	vont

AVOIR   to have
Past participle: eu; Commands: Aie! Ayez!

Subj.	Present	Subj.	Present
je	ai	nous	avons
tu	as	vous	avez
il	a	ils	ont

BOIRE   to drink
Past participle: bu; Commands: Bois! Buvez!

Subj.	Present	Subj.	Present
je	bois	nous	buvons
tu	bois	vous	buvez
il	boit	ils	boivent

CONNAÎTRE   to know
Past participle: connu; Commands: Connais! Connaissez!

Subj.	Present	Subj.	Present
je	connais	nous	connaissons
tu	connais	vous	connaissez
il	connaît	ils	connaissent

DEVOIR   to have to
Past participle: dû; Commands: Dois! Devez!

Subj.	Present	Subj.	Present
je	dois	nous	devons
tu	dois	vous	devez
il	doit	ils	doivent

DIRE   to say, tell
Past participle: dit; Commands: Dis! Dites!

Subj.	Present	Subj.	Present
je	dis	nous	disons
tu	dis	vous	dites
il	dit	ils	disent

ÉCRIRE   to write
Past participle: écrit; Commands: Écris! Écrivez!

Subj.	Present	Subj.	Present
je	écris	nous	écrivons
tu	écris	vous	écrivez
il	écrit	ils	écrivent

ÊTRE   to be
Past participle: été; Commands: Sois! Soyez!

Subj.	Present	Subj.	Present
je	suis	nous	sommes
tu	es	vous	e[ac]tes
il	est	ils	sont

FAIRE   to make, do
Past participle: fait; Commands: Fais! Faites!

Subj.	Present	Subj.	Present
je	fais	nous	faisons
tu	fais	vous	faites
il	fait	ils	font

LIRE   to read
Past participle: lu; Commands: Lis! Lisez!

Subj.	Present	Subj.	Present
je	lis	nous	lisons
tu	lis	vous	lisez
il	lit	ils	lisent

METTRE   to put
Past participle: mis; Commands: Mets! Mettez!

Subj.	Present	Subj.	Present
je	mets	nous	mettons
tu	mets	vous	mettez
il	met	ils	mettent

OUVRIR   to open
Past participle: ouvert; Commands: Ouvre! Ouvrez!

Subj.	Present	Subj.	Present
je	ouvre	nous	ouvrons
tu	ouvres	vous	ouvrez
il	ouvre	ils	ouvrent

PARTIR to leave *
Past participle: parti; Commands: Pars! Partez!

Subj.	Present	Subj.	Present
je	pars	nous	partons
tu	pars	vous	partez
il	part	ils	partent

POUVOIR to be able to, can
Past participle: pu

Subj.	Present	Subj.	Present
je	peux	nous	pouvons
tu	peux	vous	pouvez
il	peut	ils	peuvent

PRENDRE to take
Past participle: pris; Commands: Prends! Prenez!

Subj.	Present	Subj.	Present
je	prends	nous	prenons
tu	prends	vous	prenez
il	prend	ils	prennent

RECEVOIR to receive
Past participle: reçu; Commands: Reçois! Recevez!

Subj.	Present	Subj.	Present
je	reçois	nous	recevons
tu	reçois	vous	recevez
il	reçoit	ils	reçoivent

SAVOIR   to know
Past participle: su; Commands: Sache! Sachiez!

Subj.	Present	Subj.	Present
je	sais	nous	savons
tu	sais	vous	savez
il	sait	ils	savent

SORTIR   to go out *
Past participle: sorti; Commands: Sors! Sortez!

Subj.	Present	Subj.	Present
je	sors	nous	sortons
tu	sors	vous	sortez
il	sort	ils	sortent

VENIR   to come *
Past participle: venu; Commands: Viens! Venez!

Subj.	Present	Subj.	Present
je	viens	nous	venons
tu	viens	vous	venez
il	vient	ils	viennent

VOIR   to see
Past participle: vu; Commands: Vois! Voyez!

Subj.	Present	Subj.	Present
je	vois	nous	voyons
tu	vois	vous	voyez
il	voit	ils	voient

VOULOIR to want

Past participle: voulu; Commands: Veuille! Veuillez!

Subj.	Present	Subj.	Present
je	veux	nous	voulons
tu	veux	vous	voulez
il	veut	ils	veulent

French-English Dictionary

French	Pronunciation	English
à	*ah*	to, at
aider	*eh-day*	to help
ail *m.*	*ahy*	garlic
aimer	*eh-may*	to like, love
alcool *m.*	*ahl-kohl*	alcohol
aliments *m.*	*ah-lee-mahN*	food
Allemagne *f.*	*ahl-mah-nyuh*	Germany
aller	*ah-lay*	to go
alors	*ah-lohrs*	then
ami *m.*	*ah-mee*	friend
an *m.*	*ahN*	year
Angleterre *f.*	*ahN-gluh-tehr*	England
année *f.*	*ah-nay*	year
annuaire *m.*	*ah-new-ehr*	telephone book
août *m.*	*oo(t)*	August
apporter	*ah-pohr-tay*	to bring
après	*ah-preh*	after, afterward
argent *m.*	*ahr-zhahN*	silver, money
arrêt de bus *m.*	*ah-reh duh bews*	bus stop
ascenseur *m.*	*ah-sahN-suhr*	elevator
assez de	*ah-say duh*	enough
assiette *f.*	*ah-syeht*	dinner plate
atelier *m.*	*ah-tuh-lyay*	studio
attendre	*ah-tahNdr*	to wait (for)
atterrir	*ah-teh-reer*	to land (plane)
au	*o*	to the
au fond (de)	*o fohN (duh)*	at the bottom (back) (of)

French	Pronunciation	English
au haut (de)	*o o (duh)*	in (at) the top (of)
au lieu (de)	*o lyuh (duh)*	instead (of)
au-dessous de	*o duh-soo de*	beneath, below
au-dessus de	*o duh-sew duh*	above, over
aujourd'hui *m.*	*oh-zhoor-dwee*	today
aussi	*o-see*	also, too
automne *m.*	*o-tohn*	autumn, fall
aux	*o*	to the
avant	*ah-vahN*	before
avertissement *m.*	*ah-vehr-tees-mahN*	warning
avion *m.*	*ah-vyohN*	airplane
avoir	*ah-vwahr*	to have
avoir besoin (de)	*ah-vwahr buh-zwaN (duh)*	need
avoir chaud	*ah-vwahr sho*	to be hot (person)
avoir envie (de)	*ah-vwahr ahN-vee (duh)*	to need
avoir faim	*ah-vwahr faN*	to be hungry
avoir froid	*ah-vwahr frwah*	to be cold (person)
avoir lieu	*ah-vwahr lyuh*	to take place
avoir mal à	*ah-vwahr mahl ah*	to have an ache in
avoir peur (de)	*ah-vwahr puhr (duh)*	to be afraid (of)
avoir raison	*ah-vwahr reh-zohN*	to be right
avoir soif	*ah-vwahr swahf*	to be thirsty
avoir sommeil	*ah-vwahr soh-mehy*	to be sleepy
avoir tort	*ah-vwahr tohr*	to be wrong
avoir … ans	*ah-vwahr…ahN*	to be…years old
avril *m.*	*ah-vreel*	April
bateau *m.*	*bah-to*	boat
beau (belle)	*bo (behl)*	handsome, beautiful
beaucoup (de)	*bo-koo (duh)*	much
beurre *m.*	*buhr*	butter
bien	*byaN*	well
bien sûr	*byaN sewr*	of course
bientôt	*byaN-to*	soon
bière *f.*	*byehr*	beer
bifteck *m.*	*beef-tehk*	steak
bijouterie *f.*	*bee-zhoo-tree*	jewelry store
billet *m.*	*bee-yeh*	ticket

French	Pronunciation	English
blanc(he)	*blahN(sh)*	white
blanchisserie *f.*	*blahN-shees-ree*	laundry and dry cleaning service
bleu	*bluh*	blue, very rare
boeuf *m.*	*buhf*	beef
boire	*bwahr*	to drink
boisson *f.*	*bwah-sohN*	drink
boîte *f.*	*bwaht*	box, can
boîte de nuit *f.*	*bwaht duh nwee*	nightclub
bol *m.*	*bohl*	bowl
bon marché	*bohN mahr-shay*	cheap
bon(ne)	*bohN (bohn)*	good
bonbon *m.*	*bohN-bohN*	candy
bonjour	*bohN-zhoor*	hello
bonsoir	*bohN swahr*	good evening
boucher (bouchère)	*boo-shay (boo-shehr)*	butcher
boulanger (-ère)	*boo-lahn-zhay (zhehr)*	baker
bouteille *f.*	*boo-tehy*	bottle
briquet *m.*	*bree-keh*	lighter
brosse *f.*	*brohs*	brush
brosse à dents *f.*	*brohs ah dahN*	toothbrush
brouillard *m.*	*broo-yahr*	fog
brun	*bruhN*	brown, brunette
bureau de change *m.*	*bew-ro duh shahNzh*	money exchange
bureau de tabac *m.*	*bew-ro duh tah-bah*	tobacconist
c'est	*seh*	it is
c'est entendu	*seh tahN-tahN-dew*	it's understood, agreed, all right
c'est-à-dire	*seh-tah-deer*	that is to say
ça	*sah*	that
ça va	*sah vah*	okay
caisse *f.*	*kehs*	cashier
canard *m.*	*kah-nard*	duck
carte *f.*	*kahrt*	menu, card
carte postale *f.*	*kahrt pohs-tahl*	post card
ce	*suh*	this, that
ceinture *f.*	*saN-tewr*	belt
cela	*suh-lah*	that

French	Pronunciation	English
cent	*sahN*	hundred
cerise *m.*	*suh-reez*	cherry
ces	*say*	these, those
cet	*seht*	this, that
cette	*seht*	this, that
chaise *f.*	*shehz*	chair
champignon *m.*	*shahN-pee-nyohN*	mushroom
chapeau *m.*	*shah-po*	hat
charcuterie *f.*	*shahr-kew-tree*	delicatessen
chariot *m.*	*shah-ryoh*	cart
chaussettes *f.*	*sho-seht*	socks
chaussures *f.*	*sho-sewr*	shoes
chemise *f.*	*shuh-meez*	shirt (man-tailored)
chemisier *m.*	*shuh-meez-yay*	blouse
cher (chère)	*shehr*	dear, expensive
chercher	*shehr-shay*	to look for
cheveux *m. pl.*	*shuh-vuh*	hair
chez	*shay*	at the house (business) of
choisir	*shwah-zeer*	to choose
chouette	*shoo-eht*	great
cinq	*saNk*	five
cinquante	*saN-kahNt*	fifty
cintre *m.*	*saNtr*	hanger
ciseaux *m.*	*see-zo*	scissors
citron *m.*	*see-trohN*	lemon
citron pressé *m.*	*see-trohN preh-say*	lemonade
clé (clef)	*klay (klay)*	key
coffre *m.*	*kohfr*	trunk, safe (deposit box)
coiffeur (coiffeuse)	*kwah-fuhr (kwah-fuhz)*	hairdresser
combien (de + noun)	*kohN-byaN (duh)*	how much, many
comme	*kohm*	as
commencer (à)	*koh-mahN-say (ah)*	to begin
comment	*kohN-mahN*	how
comprendre	*kohN-prahNdr*	to understand
confiserie *f.*	*kohN-feez-ree*	candy store
confiture *f.*	*kohN-fee-tewr*	jam, jelly

French	Pronunciation	English
connaître	*koh-nehtr*	to be acquainted with
court	*koor*	short
couteau *m.*	*koo-to*	knife
coûter	*koo-tay*	to cost
couverture *f.*	*koo-vehr-tewr*	blanket
cravate *f.*	*krah-vaht*	tie
crayon *m.*	*kreh-yohN*	pencil
crevette *f.*	*kruh-veht*	shrimp
cuir *m.*	*kweer*	leather
d'accord	*dah-kohr*	agreed, okay
d'ailleurs	*dah-yuhr*	besides, moreover
dans	*dahN*	in
de	*duh*	from, of, about, any
de bonne heure	*duh bohn uhr*	early
décollage *m.*	*day-koh-lahzh*	takeoff
défendre	*day-fahNdr*	to defend, prohibit
déjà	*day-zhah*	already
déjeuner *m.*	*day-zhuh-nay*	to eat lunch
demain *m.*	*duh-maN*	tomorrow
dentifrice *m.*	*dahN-tee-frees*	mouthwash/toothpaste
dépenser	*day-pahN-say*	spend (money)
depuis	*duh-pwee*	since
dernier (-ère)	*dehr-nyah (nyehr)*	last
derrière	*dehr-ryehr*	behind
des	*day*	from, of, about (the), some
deux	*duh*	two
devant	*duh-vahN*	in front of
devoir	*duh-vwahr*	to have to
dimanche *m.*	*dee-mahNsh*	Sunday
dinde *f.*	*daNd*	turkey
dire	*deer*	to say, tell
dix	*dees*	ten
dix-huit	*deez-weet*	eighteen
dix-neuf	*deez-nuhf*	nineteen
dix-sept	*dee-seht*	seventeen
donner	*doh-nay*	to give
dormir	*dohr-meer*	to sleep

French	Pronunciation	English
douane *f.*	*doo-ahn*	customs
douche *f.*	*doosh*	shower
douze	*dooz*	twelve
du	*dew*	from, of, about (the), some
écouter	*ay-koo-tay*	to listen (to)
écrire	*ay-kreer*	to write
église *f.*	*ay gleez*	church
elle	*ehl*	she, her
elles	*ehl*	they, them
en	*ahN*	some, about, from, of it, them
encore	*ahN-kohr*	still, yet, again
enfant *m./f.*	*ahN-fahN*	child
enfin	*ahN-faN*	finally, at last
enlever	*ahN-lvay*	to take off, remove
ensemble	*ahN-sahNbl*	together
ensuite	*ahN-sweet*	then, afterward
entendre	*ahN-tahNdr*	to hear
entier (-ère)	*ahN-tyay (yehr)*	entire
entre	*ahNtr*	between
envoyer	*ahN-vwah-yay*	to send
épicier (-ère)	*ay-pee-syay (yehr)*	grocer
escale *f.*	*ehs-kahl*	stopover
escalier *m.*	*ehs-kah-lyay*	stairs
Espagne *f.*	*ehs-pah-nyuh*	Spain
espérer	*ehs-pay-ray*	to hope
essayer (de)	*eh-say-yay (duh)*	to try (to)
essence *f.*	*eh-sahNs*	gasoline
est *m.*	*ehst*	east
étage *m.*	*ay-tahzh*	floor (story)
Etats-Unis *m.*	*ay-tah zew-nee*	United States
été *m.*	*ay-tay*	summer
étiquette *f.*	*ay-tee-keht*	identification tag
étranger (-ère)	*ay-trahN-zhay (yehr)*	foreign
être	*ehtr*	to be
eux	*uh*	them
facile	*fah-seel*	easy
faire	*fehr*	to make, do

French	Pronunciation	English
faux (fausse)	*fo (fos)*	false
femme *f.*	*fahm*	woman, wife
fenêtre *f.*	*fuh-nehtr*	window
fermer	*fehr-may*	to close
fêter	*feh-tay*	to celebrate
février *m.*	*fay-vree-yay*	February
fille *f.*	*fee-y*	daughter, girl
fils *m.*	*fees*	son
finir	*fee-neer*	to finish
fourchette *f.*	*foor-sheht*	fork
frais (fraîche)	*freh (frehsh)*	fresh
fraise *f.*	*frehz*	strawberry
framboise *f.*	*frahN-bwahz*	raspberry
français	*frahN-seh*	French
frère *m.*	*frehr*	brother
fromage *m.*	*froh-mahzh*	cheese
fruits de mer *m. pl.*	*frwee duh mehr*	seafood
fumer	*few-may*	to smoke
gagner	*gah-nyay*	to win, earn
garçon *m.*	*gahr-sohN*	boy, waiter
gâteau *m.*	*gah-to*	cake
gazeux (-euse)	*gah-zuh(z)*	carbonated
gérant *m.*	*zhay-rahN*	manager
glace *f.*	*glahs*	ice cream, mirror
glaçons *m.*	*glah-sohN*	ice cubes
grand	*grahN*	big
gris	*gree*	gray
guichet *m.*	*gee-sheh*	window
heure *f.*	*uhr*	hour
hier	*yehr*	yesterday
hiver *m.*	*ee-vehr*	winter
homard *m.*	*oh-mahr*	lobster
homme *m.*	*ohm*	man
huit	*weet*	eight
huître *f.*	*weetr*	oyster
hypermarché *m.*	*ee-pehr-mahr-shay*	large supermarket
ici	*ee-see*	here
il	*eel*	he

French	Pronunciation	English
il y a (+ time)	*eel yah*	there is, are; ago (+ time)
ils	*eel*	they
immeuble *m.*	*ee-muhbl*	apartment building
imperméable *m.*	*aN-pehr-may-ahbl*	raincoat
jamais	*zhah-meh*	never, ever
jambon *m.*	*zhahN-bohN*	ham
janvier *m.*	*zhahN-vyay*	January
jaune	*zhon*	yellow
je	*zhuh*	I
jeudi *m.*	*zhuh-dee*	Thursday
joli	*zhoh-lee*	pretty
jouer	*zhoo-ay*	to play, gamble
jour *m.*	*zhoor*	day
journal *m.*	*zhoor-nahl*	newspaper
juillet *m.*	*zhwee-eh*	July
juin *m.*	*zhwaN*	June
jupe *f.*	*zhewp*	skirt
jus de *m.* (+ name of fruit)	*zhew duh*	fruit juice
kiosk à journaux *m.*	*kee-ohsk ah zhoor-noh*	newsstand
la	*lah*	the, her, it
là	*lah*	there
laisser	*leh-say*	to leave (behind)
lait *m.*	*leh*	milk
laitue *f.*	*leh-tew*	lettuce
laquelle	*lah-kehl*	which one
le	*luh*	the, him, it
légume *m.*	*lay-gewm*	vegetable
lentement	*lahNt-mahN*	slowly
lequelle	*luh-kehl*	which one
les	*lay*	the, them
lettre *f.*	*lehtr*	letter
leurs	*luhr*	their
librairie *f.*	*lee-breh-ree*	bookstore
lire	*leer*	to read
lit *m.*	*lee*	bed
livre *m.*	*leevr*	book

French	Pronunciation	English
location de voitures *f.*	*loh-kah-syohN duh vwah-tewr*	car rental
loin (de)	*lwaN (duh)*	far (from)
longtemps	*lohN-tahN*	a long time
louer	*loo-ay*	to rent
lourd	*loor*	heavy
lui	*lwee*	him, to him, her
lundi *m.*	*luhN-dee*	Monday
lunettes de soleil *f. pl.*	*lew-neht duh soh-lehy*	sunglasses
magasin *m.*	*mah-gah-zaN*	store
mai *m.*	*meh*	May
maillot de bain *m.*	*mah-yod baN*	bathing suit
main *f.*	*maN*	hand
maintenant	*maNt-nahN*	now
maison *f.*	*meh-zohN*	house
malade	*mah-lahd*	sick
manger	*mahN-zhay*	to eat
manteau *m.*	*mahN-to*	overcoat
maquillage *m.*	*mah-kee-yahzh*	makeup
mardi *m.*	*mahr-dee*	Tuesday
mari *m.*	*mah-ree*	husband
maroquinerie *f.*	*mah-roh-kaN-ree*	leather goods store
mars *m.*	*mahrs*	March
mauvais	*mo-veh*	bad
me	*muh*	me, to me
médecin *m.*	*mayd-saN*	doctor
médicament *m.*	*may-dee-kah-mahN*	medicine
meilleur	*meh-yuhr*	better
même	*mehm*	even
mer *f.*	*mehr*	sea
mercredi *m.*	*mehr-kruh-dee*	Wednesday
mère *f.*	*mehr*	mother
mes	*may*	my
météo *f.*	*may-tay-o*	weather
métro *m.*	*may-tro*	subway
mettre	*mehtr*	put (on)
midi *m.*	*mee-dee*	noon
mieux	*myuh*	better

French	Pronunciation	English
mille *m.*	*meel*	thousand
minuit *m.*	*mee-nwee*	midnight
moi	*mwah*	me, I
moins	*mwaN*	less
mois	*mwah*	month
monter	*mohN-tay*	to go up
montre *f.*	*mohNtr*	watch
montrer	*mohN-tray*	to show
musée *m.*	*mew-zay*	museum
n'est-ce pas	*nehs-pah*	isn't that so
n'importe	*naN-pohrt*	it doesn't matter
ne ... jamais	*nuh ... zhah-meh*	never
ne ... plus	*nuh ... plew*	no longer
ne ... rien	*nuh ... ryaN*	nothing, anything
neige *f.*	*nehzh*	snow
nettoyer	*neh-twah-yay*	to clean
neuf	*nuhf*	nine
noir(e)	*nwahr*	black
noix *f.*	*nwah*	walnut
nord *m.*	*nohr*	north
nos	*no*	our
notre	*nohtr*	our
nous	*noo*	we, us, to us
nouveau (nouvelle)	*noo-vo (noo-vehl)*	new
novembre *m.*	*noh-vahNbr*	November
nuage *m.*	*new-ahzh*	cloud
objets trouvés *m.*	*ohb-zheh troo-vay*	lost and found
octobre *m.*	*ohk-tohbr*	October
oeuf *m.*	*uhf*	eggs
oignon *m.*	*oh-nyohN*	onion
on	*ohN*	one, we, they, you
onze	*ohNz*	eleven
or *m.*	*ohr*	gold
orage *m.*	*oh-rahzh*	storms
où	*oo*	where
ouest *m.*	*wehst*	west
ouvert	*oo-vehr*	open
pain *m.*	*paN*	bread
pantalon *m.*	*pahN-tah-lohN*	pants

French	Pronunciation	English
par	*pahr*	by, through, per
parapluie *m.*	*pah-rah-plwee*	umbrella
parfois	*pahr-fwah*	sometimes
parler	*pahr-lay*	to speak
partir	*pahr-teer*	to leave
pendant	*pahN-dahN*	during
penser (à) (de)	*pahN-say (ah) (duh)*	to think (about) (of)
perdre	*pehrdr*	lose
père *m.*	*pehr*	father
petit	*puh-tee*	small
peu (de)	*puh (duh)*	little
piscine *f.*	*pee-seen*	swimming pool
plage *f.*	*plahzh*	beach
pluie *f.*	*plwee*	rain
plus	*plew*	more
pneu *m.*	*pnuh*	tire
poisson *m.*	*pwah-sohN*	fish
poivre *m.*	*pwahvr*	pepper
pomme *f.*	*pohm*	apple
pomme de terre *f.*	*pohm duh tehr*	potato
porte *f.*	*pohrt*	door, gate
portefeuille *m.*	*pohr-tuh-fuhy*	wallet
porter	*pohr-tay*	wear, carry
portier *m.*	*pohr-tyay*	doorman
poulet *m.*	*poo-leh*	chicken
pour	*poor*	for, in order to
pourquoi	*poor-kwah*	why
pouvoir	*poo-vwahr*	to be able to
premier (-ère)	*pruh-myay (yehr)*	first
prendre	*prahNdr*	to take
près (de)	*preh (duh)*	near
presque	*prehsk*	almost
prêter	*preh-tay*	to lend
printemps *m.*	*praN-tahN*	spring
prix *m.*	*pree*	price
prochain	*proh-shahN*	next
propre	*prohpr*	clean
puis	*pwee*	then
qu'est-ce que	*kehs-kuh*	what

French	Pronunciation	English
quand	*kahN*	when
quarante	*kah-rahNt*	forty
quatorze	*kah-tohrz*	fourteen
quatre	*kahtr*	four
quatre-vingt-dix	*kahtr-vaN-dees*	ninety
quatre-vingts	*kahtr-vaN*	eighty
que	*kuh*	that, what
quel(le)(s)	*kehl*	which, what
quelquefois	*kehl-kuh-fwah*	sometimes
qui	*kee*	who, whom
quinze	*kaNz*	fifteen
recevoir	*ruh-suh-vwahr*	to receive
reçu *m.*	*ruh-sew*	receipt
regarder	*ruh-gahr-day*	to look at, watch
rencontrer	*rahN-kohN-tray*	to meet
rendre	*rahNdr*	to give back, return
renseignements *m.*	*rahN-seh-nyuh-mahN*	information
rentrer	*rahN-tray*	to return
répéter	*ray-pay-tay*	to repeat
répondre (à)	*ray-pohNdr (ah)*	to answer
rester	*rehs-tay*	to stay, remain
rez-de-chaussée *m.*	*rayd-sho-say*	ground floor
robe *f.*	*rohb*	dress
rouge	*roozh*	red
sa	*sah*	his, her
sac (à main) *m.*	*sahk (ah maN)*	pocketbook
salle *f.*	*sahl*	room
saluer	*sah-lew-ay*	greet
salut	*sah-lew*	hi
samedi *m.*	*sahm-dee*	Saturday
sans	*sahN*	without
sans doute	*sahN doot*	without a doubt
savoir	*sah-vwahr*	to know
savon *m.*	*sah-vohN*	soap
se	*suh*	to him (her) (them) self (selves)
seize	*sehz*	sixteen
sel *m.*	*sehl*	salt
semaine *f.*	*suh-mehn*	week

French	Pronunciation	English
sembler	*sahN-blay*	seem
sept	*seht*	seven
septembre *m.*	*sehp-tahNbr*	September
ses	*say*	his, her
seulement	*suhl-mahN*	only
siège *m.*	*syehzh*	chair, seat
six	*sees*	six
soeur *f.*	*suhr*	sister
soi	*swah*	oneself
soixante	*swah-sahNt*	sixty
soixante-dix	*swah-sahNt-dees*	seventy
soleil *m.*	*soh-lehy*	sun
son	*sohN*	his, her
sortie *f.*	*sohr-tee*	exit
sortie de secours *f.*	*sohr-tee duh suh-koor*	emergency exit
sortir	*sohr-teer*	to go out
souhaiter	*soo-eh-tay*	to wish
souliers *m.*	*soo-lyay*	shoes
sous	*soo*	under
sous-sol *m.*	*soo-sohl*	basement
souvent	*soo-vahN*	often
sucre *m.*	*sewkr*	sugar
sud *m.*	*sewd*	south
sur	*sewr*	on
sympathique	*saN-pah-teek*	nice
ta	*tah*	your (fam.)
tailleur *m.*	*tah-yuhr*	tailor, suit
tard	*tahr*	late
tarif *m.*	*tah-reef*	price, rate
te	*tuh*	you, to you
tempête *f.*	*tahN-peht*	storm
terre *f.*	*tehr*	land
tes	*tay*	your (fam.)
timbre *m.*	*taNbr*	stamp
tirer	*tee-ray*	to pull, shoot
toi	*twah*	you
ton	*tohN*	your (fam.)
tôt	*to*	soon, early
toujours	*too-zhoor*	always, still

French	Pronunciation	English
tout	*too*	quite, entirely, all, every
tout de suite	*toot sweet*	immediately
travailler	*trah-vah-yay*	to work
traverser	*trah-vehr-say*	to cross
treize	*trehz*	thirteen
trente	*trahNt*	thirty
très	*treh*	very
trois	*trwah*	three
trop (de)	*tro (duh)*	too much, too many
trouver	*troo-vay*	to find
tu	*tew*	you
un, une	*uhN, ewn*	one
valoir	*vah-lwahr*	to be worth
veau *m.*	*vo*	veal
veille *f.*	*vehy*	eve
vendredi *m.*	*vahN-druh-dee*	Friday
vent *m.*	*vaN*	wind
verre *m.*	*vehr*	lens, glass
vers	*vehr*	toward
vert	*vehr*	green
vêtements *m.*	*veht-mahN*	clothing
viande *f.*	*vyahNd*	meat
vide	*veed*	empty
vieux (vieille)	*vyuh (vyay)*	old
vin *m.*	*vaN*	wine
vingt	*vaN*	twenty
vite	*veet*	quickly
voir	*vwahr*	to see
voiture *f.*	*vwah-tewr*	car
vol *m.*	*vohl*	flight
volaille *f.*	*voh-lahy*	poultry
vos	*vo*	your (pol.)
votre	*vohtr*	your (pol.)
vouloir	*voo-lwahr*	to want
vous	*voo*	you, to you
vraiment	*vreh-mahN*	really, truly
y	*ee*	there

English-French Dictionary

English	French	Pronunciation
A.M.	du matin	*dew mah-taN*
to able, be … to	pouvoir	*poo-vwahr*
about (the)	de (du, de la, de l')	*duh (dew, duh lah, duh l)*
above	au-dessus de	*o duh-sew de*
across	à travers	*ah trah-vehr*
ad	annonce	*ah-nohNs*
	publicitaire *f.*	*pew-blee-see-tehr*
afraid, be … (of)	avoir peur (de)	*ah-vwahr puhr (duh)*
after	après	*ah-preh*
afternoon (in the)	après-midi *m.* (de l')	*duh lah-preh mee-dee (del)*
afterward	après, ensuite	*ah-preh, ahN-sweet*
again	encore	*ahN-kohr*
against	contre	*kohNtr*
ago (+ time)	il y a (+ time)	*eel yah*
to agree (with)	être d'accord (avec)	*ehtr dah-kohr (ah-vehk)*
air conditioning	climatisation *f.*	*klee-mah-tee-zah-syohN*
air letter	aérogramme *m.*	*ahy-roh-grahm*
airline	ligne aérienne *f.*	*lee-nyuh ahy-ryehn*
airplane	avion *m.*	*ah-vyohN*
airport	aéroport *m.*	*ahy-roh-pohr*
all	tout	*too*
almost	presque	*prehsk*
already	déjà	*day-zhah*
also	aussi	*o-see*
always	toujours	*too-zhoor*
to answer	répondre (à)	*ray-pohNdr (ah)*
any	de	*duh*
apple	pomme *f.*	*pohm*
April	avril *m.*	*ah-vreel*

English	French	Pronunciation
area code	indicatif *m.*	*aN-dee-kah-teef*
to arrive	arriver	*ah-ree-vay*
ashtray	cendrier *m.*	*sahN-dree-yay*
to ask	demander	*duh-mahN-day*
aspirin	aspirine *f.*	*ah-spee-reen*
at	à	*ah*
August	août *m.*	*oo(t)*
autumn	automne *m.*	*o-tohn*
bad	mauvais	*mo-veh*
baggage claim area	bagages *m.*	*bah-gahzh*
bakery	boulangerie *f.*	*boo-lahNzh-ree*
ball-point pen	stylo à bille *m.*	*stee-lo ah bee-y*
band-aid	pansement adhésif *m.*	*pahNs-mahN ahd-ay-zeef*
bathing suit	maillot de bain *m.*	*mah-yod baN*
bathroom	toilettes *f.*,	*twah-leht*
to be	être	*ehtr*
beach	plage *f.*	*plahzh*
beautiful	beau (belle)	*bo (behl)*
bed	lit *m.*	*lee*
beef	boeuf *m.*	*buhf*
beer	bière *f.*	*byehr*
before	avant	*ah-vahN*
to begin	commencer (à)	*koh-mahN-say (ah)*
behind	derrière, en arrière	*deh-ryehr, ahN nah-ryehr*
to belong to	être à	*ehtr ah*
below	au-dessous de	*o duh-soo de*
belt	ceinture *f.*	*saN-tewr*
better	meilleur, mieux	*meh-yuhr, myuh*
between	entre	*ahNtr*
big	grand, gros(se)	*grahN, gro(s)*
black	noir(e)	*nwahr*
blanket	couverture *f.*	*koo-vehr-tewr*
blouse	chemisier *m.*	*shuh-meez-yay*
blue	bleu	*bluh*
boat	bateau *m.*	*bah-to*
book	livre *m.*	*leevr*
bookstore	librairie *f.*	*lee-breh-ree*

English	French	Pronunciation
boot	botte *f.*	*boht*
booth (telephone)	cabine téléphonique *f.*	*kah-been tay-lay-foh-neek*
bowl	bol *m.*	*bohl*
box	boîte *f.*	*bwaht*
boy	garçon *m.*	*gahr-sohN*
bread	pain *m.*	*paN*
to bring (person)	amener	*ahm-nay*
to bring (thing)	apporter	*ah-pohr-tay*
to bring back	remporter	*rahN-pohr-tay*
brother	frère *m.*	*frehr*
brown	brun	*bruhN*
brush	brosse *f.*	*brohs*
bus stop	arrêt de bus *m.*	*ah-reh duh bews*
business center	centre d'affaires *m.*	*sahNtr dah-fehr*
butcher shop	boucherie *f.*	*boosh-ree*
butter	beurre *m.*	*buhr*
button	bouton *m.*	*boo-tohN*
by	par	*pahr*
cake	gâteau *m.*	*gah-to*
camera	appareil-photo *m.*	*ah-pah-rehy foh-to*
can	boîte *f.*	*bwaht*
candy	bonbon *m.*	*bohN-bohN*
candy store	confiserie *f.*	*kohN-feez-ree*
car	auto *f.*, voiture *f.*	*o-to, vwah-tewr*
car rental	location de voitures *f.*	*loh-kah-syohN duh vwah-tewr*
card	carte *f.*	*kahrt*
carrot	carotte *f.*	*kah-roht*
carry	porter	*pohr-tay*
cart	chariot *m.*	*shah-ryoh*
to cash (check)	toucher	*too-shay*
cash register	caisse *f.*	*kehs*
castle	château *m.*	*shah-to*
chair	chaise *f.*, siège *m.*	*shehz, syehzh*
cheese	fromage *m.*	*froh-mahzh*
chicken	poule *f.*, poulet *m.*	*pool, poo-leh*
child	enfant *m./f.*	*ahN-fahN*
to choose	choisir	*shwah-zeer*

English	French	Pronunciation
church	église *f.*	*ay gleez*
to clean	propre	*prohpr*
to close	fermer	*fehr-may*
clothing	vêtements *m.*	*veht-mahN*
coffee	café *m.*	*kah-fay*
cold	rhume *m.*	*rewm*
comb	peigne *m.*	*peh-nyuh*
contact lens	lentille *f.* de contact, verre *m.* de contact	*lahN-tee-y duh kohN-tahkt, vehr duh kohN-tahkt*
cookie	biscuit *m.*	*bees-kwee*
cooking	cuisine *f.*	*kwee-zeen*
corner	coin *m.*	*kwaN*
to cost	coûter	*koo-tay*
cough drops	pastilles *f.*	*pahs-tee-y*
cough syrup	sirop contre la toux *m.*	*see-roh kohNtr lah too*
counter	comptoir *m.*	*kohN-twahr*
cup	tasse *f.*	*tahss*
customs	douane *f.*	*doo-ahn*
dark	foncé	*fohN-say*
daughter	fille *f.*	*fee-y*
day	jour *m.*	*zhoor*
day after tomorrow	après-demain *m.*	*ah-preh duh-maN*
day before yesterday	avant-hier	*ah-vahN yehr*
December	décembre *m.*	*day-sahNbr*
delicatessen	charcuterie *f.*	*shahr-kew-tree*
department store	grand magasin *m.*	*grahN mah-gah-zaN*
departure	départ *m.*	*day-pahr*
deposit box	coffre *m.*	*kohfr*
to dine	dîner	*dee-nay*
dirty	sale	*sahl*
to disturb	déranger	*day-rahN-zhay*
to do	faire	*fehr*
doctor	docteur *m.*, médecin *m.*	*dohk-tuhr, mayd-saN*
dog	chien *m.*	*shyaN*
door	porte *f.*	*pohrt*

English	French	Pronunciation
downtown	en ville	*ahN veel*
dozen	une douzaine de	*ewn doo-zehn duh*
dress	robe *f.*	*rohb*
to drink	boire	*bwahr*
drink	boisson *f.*	*bwah-sohN*
to dry clean	nettoyer à sec	*neh-twah-yay ah sehk*
dry cleaner's	teinturerie *f.*	*taN-tew-ruh-ree*
during	pendant	*pahN-dahN*
ear	oreille *f.*	*oh-rehy*
early	de bonne heure, tôt	*duh bohn uhr, to*
to earn	gagner	*gah-nyay*
earrings	boucles *f.* d'oreille	*bookl doh-rehy*
east	est *m.*	*ehst*
easy	facile	*fah-seel*
to eat	manger	*mahN-zhay*
egg	oeuf *m.*	*uhf*
eight	huit	*weet*
eighteen	dix-huit	*deez-weet*
eighty	quatre-vingts	*kahtr-vaN*
elevator	ascenseur *m.*	*ah-sahN-suhr*
eleven	onze	*ohNz*
embassy	ambassade *f.*	*ahN-bah-sahd*
to end	terminer	*tehr-mee-nay*
England	Angleterre *f.*	*ahN-gluh-tehr*
enough	assez de	*ah-say duh*
to enter	entrer	*ahN-tray*
entrance	entrée *f.*	*ahN-tray*
every	tout	*too*
excuse me	pardon	*pahr-dohN*
exit	sortie *f.*	*sohr-tee*
expensive	cher (chère)	*shehr*
to explain	expliquer	*ehks-plee-kay*
eye	oeil *m.* (pl. yeux)	*uhy (yuh)*
fall	automne *m.*	*o-tohn*
fantastic	génial	*zhay-nyahl*
far (from)	loin (de)	*lwaN (duh)*
father	père *m.*	*pehr*
favorite	favori(te)	*fah-voh-ree(t)*
fax	télécopie *f.*	*tay-lay-koh-pee*

English	French	Pronunciation
February	février *m.*	*fay-vree-yay*
fifteen	quinze	*kaNz*
fifty	cinquante	*saN-kahNt*
find	trouver	*troo-vay*
to finish	achever, finir	*ah-shuh-vay, fee-neer*
fish store	poissonnerie *f.*	*pwah-sohn-ree*
five	cinq	*saNk*
floor (story)	étage *m.*	*ay-tahzh*
for	pour	*poor*
foreign	étranger (-ère)	*ay-trahN-zhay (zhehr)*
to forget	oublier	*oo-blee-yay*
fork	fourchette *f.*	*foor-sheht*
forty	quarante	*kah-rahNt*
four	quatre	*kahtr*
fourteen	quatorze	*kah-tohrz*
French	français	*frahN-seh*
fresh	frais (fraîche)	*freh (frehsh)*
Friday	vendredi *m.*	*vahN-druh-dee*
friend	ami *m.*	*ah-mee*
from	de, de la, de l', des, du, en	*duh, duh lah, duh l, day, dew, ahN*
front, in ... of	devant	*duh-vahN*
fruit store	fruiterie *f.*	*frwee-tree*
fun	amusant	*ah-mew-zahN*
funny	comique, drôle	*koh-meek, drohl*
game, to play a ... of	faire une partie de	*fehr ewn pahr-tee duh*
gasoline	essence *f.*	*eh-sahNs*
gate	porte *f.*	*pohrt*
Germany	Allemagne *f.*	*ahl-mah-nyuh*
gift shop	boutique *f.*	*boo-teek*
girl	fille *f.*	*fee-y*
give	donner	*doh-nay*
to give back	rendre	*rahNdr*
glass	verre *m.*	*vehr*
glove	gant *m.*	*gahN*
to go	aller	*ah-lay*
good	bon(ne)	*bohN (bohn)*
good-bye	au revoir	*o ruh-vwahr*

English	French	Pronunciation
gray	gris	*gree*
great	chouette, extra, formidable	*shoo-eht, ehks-trah, fohr-mee-dahbl*
green	vert	*vehr*
grocery store	épicerie *f.*	*ay-pees-ree*
ground floor	rez-de-chaussée *m.*	*rayd-sho-say*
hair	cheveux *m.*	*shuh-vuh*
haircut	coupe de cheveux *f.*	*koop duh shuh-vuh*
ham	jambon *m.*	*zhahN-bohN*
hamburger	hamburger *m.*	*ahN-bewr-gehr*
hand	main *f.*	*maN*
hanger	cintre *m.*	*saNtr*
happy	heureux (-euse)	*uh-ruh(z)*
hat	chapeau *m.*	*shah-po*
to have	avoir	*ah-vwahr*
he	il	*eel*
to hear	entendre	*ahN-tahNdr*
hello	bonjour	*bohN-zhoor*
to help	aider	*eh-day*
her (to)	elle, la, sa, son, ses, (lui)	*ehl, lah, sah, sohN, say, (lwee)*
here	ici	*ee-see*
hi	salut	*sah-lew*
him, (to)	le (lui)	*luh, (lwee)*
his	sa, son, ses	*sah, sohN, say*
hour	heure *f.*	*uhr*
house	maison *f.*	*meh-zohN*
house, at the ... (business) of	chez	*shay*
how	comment	*kohN-mahN*
how much, many	combien (de + noun)	*kohN-byaN (duh)*
hundred	cent	*sahN*
hungry, to be	avoir faim	*ah-vwahr faN*
husband	mari *m.*	*mah-ree*
I	je	*zhuh*
ice cream	glace *f.*	*glahs*
ice cubes	glaçons *m.*	*glah-sohN*
immediately	tout de suite	*toot sweet*
in	dans	*dahN*

English	French	Pronunciation
information	renseignements *m.*	*rahN-seh-nyuh-mahN*
instead (of)	au lieu (de)	*o lyuh (duh)*
to invite	inviter	*aN-vee-tay*
it	le, la	*luh, lah*
it is	c'est	*seh*
January	janvier *m.*	*zhahN-vyay*
jar	bocal *m.*	*boh-kahl*
jewelry store	bijouterie *f.*	*bee-zhoo-tree*
juice	jus *m.*, jus de + name of fruit	*zhew (duh)*
July	juillet *m.*	*zhwee-eh*
June	juin *m.*	*zhwaN*
to keep	garder	*gahr-day*
key	clé (clef) *f.*	*klay (klay)*
to know	savoir	*sah-vwahr*
to land (plane)	atterrir	*ah-teh-reer*
landing	palier *m.*	*pah-lyay*
last	dernier (-ère), passé(e)	*dehr-nyah (nyehr), pah-say*
late	tard	*tahr*
late (in arriving)	en retard	*ahN ruh-tahr*
laundry	blanchisserie *f.*	*blahN-shees-ree*
leather goods store	maroquinerie *f.*	*mah-roh-kaN-ree*
to leave (behind)	partir, quitter, (laisser)	*pahr-teer, kee-tay, (leh-say)*
left, to the … (of)	à gauche (de)	*ah gosh (duh)*
lemon	citron *m.*	*see-trohN*
lend	prêter	*preh-tay*
less	moins	*mwaN*
letter	lettre *f.*	*lehtr*
lettuce	laitue *f.*	*leh-tew*
lighter	briquet *m.*	*bree-keh*
to like	aimer	*eh-may*
to listen (to)	écouter	*ay-koo-tay*
little	peu de	*puh duh*
to live (in)	demeurer, habiter	*duh-muh-ray, ah-bee-tay*
long	long(ue)	*lohN(g)*
to look at, watch	regarder	*ruh-gahr-day*
to look for	chercher	*shehr-shay*

English	French	Pronunciation
to lose	perdre	*pehrdr*
lost and found	objets trouvés *m.*	*ohb-zheh troo-vay*
to love	aimer	*eh-may*
maid	fille de chambre *f.*	*fee-y duh shahNbr*
mailbox	boîte aux lettres *f.*	*bwaht o lehtr*
to make	faire	*fehr*
man	homme *m.*	*ohm*
manager	gérant *m.*	*zhay-rahN*
March	mars *m.*	*mahrs*
matter, it doesn't	n'importe	*naN-pohrt*
May	mai *m.*	*meh*
me, (to)	moi, me	*mwah, muh*
mechanic	mécanicien(ne)	*may-kah-nee-syaN (syehn)*
medicine	médicament *m.*	*may-dee-kah-mahN*
to meet	faire la connaissance de, rencontrer, se réunir	*fehr lah koh-neh-sahNs duh, rahN-kohN-tray, suh ray-ew-neer*
menu	carte *f.*, menu *m.*	*kahrt, muh-new*
merchandise	marchandise *f.*	*mahr-shahN-deez*
merchant	commerçant	*koh-mehr-sahN*
middle, in the … (of)	au milieu (de)	*o meel-yuh (duh)*
midnight	minuit *m.*	*nee-nwee*
milk	lait *m.*	*leh*
million	million *m.*	*meel-yohN*
mineral water carbonated non-carbonated	eau minérale *f.* gazeuse plate	*o mee-nay-rahl gah-zuhz plaht*
minute	minute *f.*	*mee-newt*
mirror	glace *f.*, miroir *m.*	*glahs, meer-wahr*
Miss	mademoiselle *f.*	*mahd-mwah-zehl*
to miss	manquer, rater	*mahN-kay, rah-tay*
mistake	faute *f.*, erreur *f.*	*foht, eh-ruhr*
Monday	lundi *m.*	*luhN-dee*
money	argent *m.*	*ahr-zhahN*
money exchange	bureau de change *m.*	*bew-ro duh shahNzh*
money order	mandat-poste *m.*	*mahN-dah pohst*
month	mois *m.*	*mwah*
more	plus	*plew*

English	French	Pronunciation
morning, (in the)	matin *m.* (du)	*mah-taN (dew)*
mother	mère *f.*	*mehr*
Mr.	monsieur *m.*	*muh-syuh*
Mrs.	madame *f.*	*mah-dahm*
much	beaucoup (de)	*bo-koo*
museum	musée *m.*	*mew-zay*
mushroom	champignon *m.*	*shahN-pee-nyohN*
mustard	moutarde *f.*	*moo-tahrd*
my	mes	*may*
napkin	serviette *f.*	*sehr-vyeht*
near	près (de)	*preh (duh)*
to need	avoir besoin (de)	*ah-vwahr buh-zwaN (duh)*
never	ne … jamais	*nuh … zhah-meh*
new	neuf, nouveau (nouvelle)	*nuhf, noo-vo (noo-vehl)*
news	informations *f.*	*aN-fohr-mah-syohN*
newspaper	journal *m.*	*zhoor-nahl*
newsstand	kiosk à journaux *m.*	*kee-ohsk ah zhoor-noh*
next	prochain	*proh-shaN*
next to, beside	à côté (de)	*ah ko-tay (duh)*
nice	aimable, gentil(le), sympathique	*eh-mahbl, zhahN-tee-y, saN-pah-teek*
night	nuit *f.*	*nwee*
nightclub	boîte de nuit *f.*, cabaret *m.*	*bwaht duh nwee, kah-bah-reh*
nine	neuf	*nuhf*
nineteen	dix-neuf	*deez-nuhf*
ninety	quatre-vingt-dix	*kahtr-vaN-dees*
no	non	*nohN*
no longer	ne … plus	*nuh … plew*
noon	midi *m.*	*mee-dee*
north	nord *m.*	*nohr*
nothing	ne … rien	*nuh … ryaN*
November	novembre *m.*	*noh-vahNbr*
now	maintenant	*maNt-nahN*
October	octobre *m.*	*ohk-tohbr*
of (the)	de, de la, de l', du, des	*duh, duh lah, duh l, dew, day*

English	French	Pronunciation
of course	bien entendu, bien sûr	*byaN nahN-tahN-dew, byaN sewr*
often	souvent	*soo-vahN*
okay	d'accord, ça va	*dah-kohr, sah vah*
on	sur	*sewr*
one	on, un, une	*ohN, uhN, ewn*
only	seulement	*suhl-mahN*
open	ouvert	*oo-vehr*
opposite	en face (de)	*ahN fahs (duh)*
orange	orange *f.*	*oh-rahNzh*
to order	commander	*koh-mahN-day*
order, in ... to	pour	*poor*
our	nos, notre	*no, nohtr*
out, to go	sortir	*sohr-teer*
P.M.	de l'après-midi	*duh lah-preh mee-dee*
package	paquet *m.*	*pah-keh*
pain	douleur *f.*	*doo-luhr*
pamphlet	brochure *f.*	*broh-shewr*
pants	pantalon *m.*	*luh pahN-tah-lohN*
paper	papier *m.*	*pah-pyay*
paper, toilet	papier hygiénique *m.*	*pah-pyay ee-zhyay-neek*
park	parc *m.*	*pahrk*
to pay, (for)	payer	*peh-yay*
pen (ball-point)	stylo à bille *m.*	*stee-lo ah beey*
pencil	crayon *m.*	*kreh-yohN*
perfume store	parfumerie *f.*	*par-fewm-ree*
phone	téléphone *m.*	*tay-lay-fohn*
pillow	oreiller *m.*	*oh-reh-yay*
pills	pilules *f. pl.*	*pee-lewl*
plate	assiette *f.*	*ah-syeht*
to play	jouer	*zhoo-ay*
please	s'il vous (te) plaît	*seel voo (tuh) pleh*
pocketbook	sac (à main) *m.*	*sahk (ah maN)*
police station	commissariat *m.* de police	*koh-mee-sah-ryah duh poh-lees*
pork	porc *m.*	*pohr*
porter	porteur *m.*	*pohr-tuhr*
post card	carte postale *f.*	*kahrt pohs-tahl*
postage	affranchissement *m.*	*ah-frahN-shees-mahN*

English	French	Pronunciation
potato	pomme de terre *f.*	*pohm duh tehr*
pound of	demi-kilo de *m.*, cinq cents grammes de	*duh-mee kee-lo duh, saNk sahN grahm duh*
prescription	ordonnance *f.*	*ohr-doh-nahNs*
pretty	joli	*zhoh-lee*
price	prix *m.*, tarif *m.*	*pree, tah-reef*
problem	problème *m.*	*proh-blehm*
to put (on)	mettre	*mehtr*
quickly	vite	*veet*
rate	tarif *m.*	*tah-reef*
receipt	quittance *f.*, reçu *m.*	*kee-tahNs, ruh-sew*
to receive	recevoir	*ruh-suh-vwahr*
red	rouge	*roozh*
to remain	rester	*rehs-tay*
to remove	enlever, ôter, quitter	*ahN-lvay, o-tay, kee-tay*
to repair	réparer	*ray-pah-ray*
to repeat	répéter	*ray-pay-tay*
to replace	remplacer	*rahN-plah-say*
to reserve	réserver	*ray-zehr-vay*
to return	rentrer, retourner	*rahN-tray, ruh-toor-nay*
to return (item)	rendre	*rahNdr*
rice	riz *m.*	*ree*
right, to be	avoir raison	*ah-vwahr reh-zohN*
right, to the (of)	à droite (de)	*ah drawht (duh)*
ring	bague *f.*	*bahg*
safe	coffre *m.*	*kohfr*
salesperson	vendeur (-euse)	*vahN-duhr (duhz)*
salt	sel *m.*	*sehl*
same, (all the)	même, (tout de même)	*mehm, (too dmehm)*
Saturday	samedi *m.*	*sahm-dee*
to say	dire	*deer*
scissors	ciseaux *m. pl.*	*see-zo*
seafood	fruits de mer *m. pl.*	*frwee duh mehr*
seat	place *f.*, siège *m.*	*plahs, syehzh*
second	deuxième, second(e)	*duhz-yehm, suh-gohN(d)*
to see	voir	*vwahr*

English	French	Pronunciation
to sell	vendre	*vahNdr*
to send	envoyer	*ahN-vwah-yay*
September	septembre *m.*	*sehp-tahNbr*
to serve	servir	*sehr-veer*
seven	sept	*seht*
seventeen	dix-sept	*dee-seht*
seventy	soixante-dix	*swah-sahNt-dees*
shampoo	shampooing *m.*	*shahN-pwaN*
she	elle	*ehl*
shirt (man-tailored)	chemise *f.*	*shuh-meez*
shoe repair person	cordonnier	*kohr-doh-nyay*
shoes	chaussures *f. pl.,* souliers *m. pl.*	*sho-sewr, soo-lyay*
shopping, to go	faire des achats (emplettes)	*fehr day zah-shah (ahN-pleht)*
short	court	*koor*
show	spectacle *m.*	*spehk-tahkl*
shower	douche *f.*	*doosh*
shrimp	crevette *f.*	*kruh-veht*
sick	malade	*mah-lahd*
to sign	signer	*see-nyay*
silk	soie *f.*	*swah*
silver	argent *m.*	*ahr-zhahN*
since	depuis	*duh-pwee*
sister	soeur *f.*	*suhr*
six	six	*sees*
sixteen	seize	*sehz*
sixty	soixante	*swah-sahNt*
size	taille *f.*	*tahy*
skirt	jupe *f.*	*zhewp*
to sleep	dormir	*dohr-meer*
slice	tranche *f.*	*trahNsh*
slide	diapositive *f.*	*dee-ah-poh-zee-teev*
slowly	lentement	*lahNt-mahN*
small	petit	*puh-tee*
to smoke	fumer	*few-may*
sneakers	tennis *f.*	*tay-nees*
soap, (bar of)	savon *m.,* (savonnette *f.*)	*sah-vohN, (sah-voh-neht)*

English	French	Pronunciation
socks	chaussettes *f.*	*sho-seht*
some	de, de la, de l', des, du	*duh, duh lah, duh l, day, dew*
sometimes	parfois, quelquefois	*pahr-fwah, kehl-kuh-fwah*
son	fils *m.*	*fees*
soon	bientôt, tôt	*byaN-to, to*
south	sud *m.*	*sewd*
souvenir shop	magasin de souvenirs *m.*	*mah-gah-zaN duh soo-vuh-neer*
Spain	Espagne *f.*	*ehs-pah-nyuh*
to speak	parler	*pahr-lay*
to spend (money)	dépenser	*day-pahN-say*
to spend (time)	passer	*pah-say*
spicy	épicé *f.*	*ay-pee-say*
spring	printemps *m.*	*praN-tahN*
stairs	escalier *m.*	*ehs-kah-lyay*
stamp	timbre *m.*	*taNbr*
stapler	agrafeuse *f.*	*ah-grah-fuhz*
stationery	papier à lettres *m.*	*pah-pyay ah lehtr*
to stay	rester	*rehs-tay*
steak	bifteck *m.*	*beef-tehk*
still	encore, toujours	*ahN-kohr, too-zhoor*
store	magasin *m.*	*mah-gah-zaN*
student	élève (*m.* or *f.*), étudiant *m.*	*ay-lehv, ay-tewd-yahN*
subway	métro *m.*	*may-tro*
sugar	sucre *m.*	*sewkr*
suitcase	valise *f.*	*vah-leez*
summer	été *m.*	*ay-tay*
Sunday	dimanche *m.*	*dee-mahNsh*
sunglasses	lunettes de soleil *f. pl.*	*lew-neht duh soh-lehy*
suntan oil	huile solaire *f.*	*weel soh-lehr*
supermarket	supermarché *m.*	*sew-pehr-mahr-shay*
sweet	doux (douce), sucré	*doo (doos), sew-kray*
to swim	nager	*nah-zhay*
Switzerland	Suisse *f.*	*swees*
table	table *f.*	*tahbl*
tailor	tailleur *m.*	*tah-yuhr*

English	French	Pronunciation
to take	prendre	*prahNdr*
to take off	enlever	*ahN-lvay*
to take place	avoir lieu	*ah-vwahr lyuh*
takeoff (plane)	décollage *m.*	*day-koh-lahzh*
tea	thé *m.*	*tay*
teaspoon	cuiller *f.*	*kwee-yehr*
telephone book	annuaire *m.*	*ah-new-wehr*
telephone number	numéro de téléphone *m.*	*new-may-ro duh tay-lay-fohn*
telephone, public	téléphone public *m.*	*tay-lay-fohn pew-bleek*
television	télévision *f.*	*tay-lay-vee-zyohN*
to tell	dire, raconter	*deer, rah-kohN-tay*
ten	dix	*dees*
that	ce, cet, cette. cela, que, ça	*suh, seht, seht, suh-lah, kuh, sah*
the	le, la, les	*luh, lah, lay*
their	leur(s)	*luhr*
them, (to)	les, elles, eux, (leur)	*lay, ehl, uh, (luhr)*
then	alors, ensuite, puis	*ah-lohrs, ahN-sweet, pwee*
there	là, y	*lah*
there is, are	il y a	*eel yah*
these	ces	*say*
they	ils, elles, on	*eel, ehl, ohN*
to think (about), (of)	penser (à), (de)	*pahN-say (ah), (duh)*
thirsty, be	avoir soif	*ah-vwahr swahf*
thirteen	treize	*trehz*
thirty	trente	*trahNt*
this	ce, cet, cette	*suh, seht, seht*
those	ces	*say*
thousand	mille *m.*	*meel*
three	trois	*trwah*
through	à travers, par	*ah trah-vehr, pahr*
Thursday	jeudi *m.*	*zhuh-dee*
ticket	billet *m.*	*bee-yeh*
time	temps *m.*, heure *f.*	*tahN, uhr*
time, a long	longtemps	*lohN-tahN*
time, at the same	à la fois, en même temps	*ah lah fwah, ahN mehm tahN*

English	French	Pronunciation
time, at what	à quelle heure	*ah kehl uhr*
time, to have the ... to	avoir le temps de	*ah-vwahr luh tahN duh*
time, on	à l'heure, à temps	*ah luhr, ah tahN*
tissue	mouchoir en papier *m.*	*moosh-wahr ahN pah-pyay*
to	à	*ah*
to the	à la, à l', au, aux	*ah lah, ah l, o, o*
today	aujourd'hui *m.*	*oh-zhoor-dwee*
together	ensemble	*ahN-sahNbl*
toilet paper	papier hygiénique *m.*	*pahp-yay ee-zhyay-neek*
token	jeton *m.*	*zheh-tohN*
tomorrow	demain *m.*	*duh-maN*
too	aussi	*o-see*
too much	trop (de)	*tro duh*
tooth	dent *f.*	*dahN*
toothache	rage *f.* de dents	*rahzh duh dahN*
toothbrush	brosse à dents *f.*	*brohs ah dahN*
toothpaste	pâte dentifrice *f.*	*paht dahN-tee-frees*
toward	vers	*vehr*
towel	serviette *f.*	*sehr-vyeht*
train	train *m.*	*traN*
transformer	transformateur *m.*	*trahNs-fohr-mah-tuhr*
to travel	voyager	*vwah-yah-zhay*
trip (to take a)	voyage *m.* (faire un)	*vwah-yahzh (fehr uhN)*
to try (to)	essayer (de)	*eh-say-yay (duh)*
Tuesday	mardi *m.*	*mahr-dee*
turkey	dinde *f.*	*daNd*
to turn	tourner	*toor-nay*
twelve	douze	*dooz*
twenty	vingt	*vaN*
two	deux	*duh*
umbrella	parapluie *m.*	*pah-rah-plwee*
under	sous	*soo*
to understand	comprendre	*kohN-prahNdr*
United States	Etats-Unis *m.*	*ay-tah zew-nee*
until	jusqu'à	*zhews-kah*
upstairs	en haut	*ahN o*

English	French	Pronunciation
us, to us	nous	*noo*
value	valeur *f.*	*vah-luhr*
vanilla	vanille *f.*	*vah-nee-y*
VCR	magnétoscope *m.*	*mah-nyay-toh-skohp*
veal	veau *m.*	*vo*
vegetable	légume *m.*	*lay-gewm*
very	très	*treh*
to wait (for)	attendre	*ah-tahNdr*
wallet	portefeuille *m.*	*pohr-tuh-fuhy*
to want	vouloir	*voo-lwahr*
watch	montre *f.*	*mohNtr*
we	nous, on	*noo, ohN*
Wednesday	mercredi *m.*	*mehr-kruh-dee*
week	semaine *f.*	*suh-mehn*
to weigh	peser	*puh-zay*
well	bien	*byaN*
west	ouest *m.*	*wehst*
what	qu'est-ce que, que, quel(le), quoi	*kehs-kuh, kuh, kehl, kwah*
when	quand	*kahN*
where	où	*oo*
which	quel(le)(s)	*kehl*
which one	lequel, laquelle	*luh-kehl, lah-kehl*
white	blanc(he)	*blahN(sh)*
who, whom	qui	*kee*
why	pourquoi	*poor-kwah*
wife	femme *f.*	*fahm*
window (ticket)	guichet *m.*	*gee-sheh*
wine	vin *m.*	*vaN*
winter	hiver *m.*	*ee-vehr*
to wish	souhaiter	*soo-eh-tay*
without	sans	*sahN*
woman	femme *f.*	*fahm*
wool	laine *f.*	*lehn*
to work	fonctionner, marcher, travailler	*fohNk-syoh-nay, mahr-shay, trah-vah-yay*
to wrap up	emballer	*ahN-bah-lay*
to write	écrire	*ay-kreer*
year	an *m.*, année *f.*	*ahN, ah-nay*

English	French	Pronunciation
years old, to be ...	avoir ... ans	*ah-vwahr ... ahN*
yellow	jaune	*zhon*
yesterday	hier	*yehr*
yet	encore	*ahN-kohr*
you, (to)	on, toi, tu, te, vous	*ohN, twah, tew, tuh, voo*
your (fam.)	ta, ton, tes	*tah, tohN, tay*
your (pol.)	vos, votre	*vo, vohtr*
zoo	zoo *m.*	*zo*

Index